Rescued Love

CULTIVATING INTIMACY IN RELATIONSHIPS

Ernesto Aragon

All Scripture quotations, unless otherwise indicated, are taken from the Holy Bible,
New International Version®, NIV®. Copyright ©1973, 1978, 1984, 2011 by Biblica,
Inc.[TM] Used by permission of Zondervan. All rights reserved worldwide.www.zonder-
van.com The "NIV" and "New International Version" are trademarks registered in the
United States Patent and Trademark Office by Biblica, Inc.[TM] Scripture quotations
marked (KJV) are taken from the Holy Bible, King James Version, KJV.

All of the stories written in this book are based on true events, but many of the names
and details of the stories have been changed to protect the privacy of the individuals.
Front Cover Art: © Zian Dinh
Rear Cover Art: © Karen Walker Designs
Rear Photo: © Breanna McMahon Photography

"Rescued Love is an inspiring book of a young man's courage to come from a place of brokenness to the only place of fullness, the very heart and love of Jesus, a place where only His love rescues the broken. Ernesto Aragon reveals his heart and all that the Lord has done in him to show him how true love heals and delivers and sets the captive free. It is a laid down life, free from walls of protection and walls of self-preservation that allows man to really know the love of God, His perfect love for His creation. Ernesto shows us through his testimony that God the Father loves us perfectly and completely, even in our weak love for Him. This book will move you to look deeper at your own heart and give God what is His, all of your perfect love for Him, no holding back."

Carolyn Figlioli
Director of Iris South Sudan and author
of "*Follow Me, Journey Into The Sudan
And Into The Heart of The Father*"

"I fell in love with Ernesto's book Rescued Love right from the introduction. Ernesto takes you on a personal journey through his life experiences of joyful and painful events that draw you in as if you were part of his story. The whole time connecting The Holy Spirit's guidance through his decisions which draw him closer to the Fathers love. Rescued Love showed me how important being a son is in our Fathers love story, and the book used plenty of scriptural references to Biblically show its points. I highly recommend this book for all readers whether you have been a Christian your entire life or you are just now turning toward God."

Ryan Hinckley
High School U.S. history teacher
and a member of the preaching
team at Destiny Life Church

"Ernesto has written a great book about his journey with God, with all of the ups and downs and messiness that life brings with it. He is not afraid to be vulnerable and share not only his successes but also those "learning moments" in life and relationships. It's an honest and transparent look in "real time," and Ernesto has done a fine job of allowing every circumstance and relational challenge to shape, influence and grow his character towards maturity. He has also found a way to incorporate Biblical truth into real life situations in a way that reframes them from an earthly to a heavenly perspective. Bravo!!!"

Mike Horn
Pastor, leader, and lifelong learner

"Ernesto Aragon is a man that has been marked by God to reveal the Father's heart! He is a true son that walks with honor and humility that is a rare gem in the church today. Rescued Love is a great book filled with the revelation of God the Father, His faithful Son, and the power of the Holy Spirit all locked within its pages."

Chris Humphrey
Burn 24-7 Sacramento
Director/Ignite Discipleship Training School

"This was a refreshing read. I Loved Ernesto's transparency. Anyone who has had struggles with their identity, addictions, pride, depression, fear, anger, & suicidal desires would totally relate to his story. As Ernesto explores his own life and shares how he overcame these issues, I believe others will experience the same freedom that he received. If you have tried to do things your way in life, but it hasn't worked... then check out this book. There are great life-giving perspectives that can help anyone no matter what they are going through."

Kathleen Michelle Le
Vice president of Awakening
The Nations, Real Life radio
show host, and ordained
minister

This book is dedicated to those of you who are struggling with depression and/or suicidal thoughts. You are not alone, and there are more people than you think who struggle with feeling isolated, alone, depressed, and purposeless. We were all created to have healthy covenant relationships with friends and family, and I believe those relationships are designed to propel us into our destiny. You were not born to survive, but you were born to change the world. We are all special, but if we were all special in the same way then nobody would be special. You are special in a way that no one else on the face of the earth is.

One of the main reasons I wrote this book is to use it as a form of suicide awareness. Suicide is not the answer to what you're going through; Jesus is the answer. No one is immune to feeling alone, and we all struggle with feeling alone from time to time. As you read this book, I pray that God will not only encounter you in a way you've never experienced before, but that you'll also get a vision for what God created you for. It's not the end, it's just the beginning.

Contents

Preface
Escaping the Pain

There I was, standing in my kitchen, holding a knife to my throat. I don't know how I got to that point in my life, but all I knew was that I wanted to end my life. A few years prior to this, I had been in a couple of relationships with women, that both ended in eerily similar ways. In both those past relationships, I had found out that there were other men who were also dating the same woman I was dating. The feeling of being rejected and immediately replaced by another man made the world look like a completely different place. But it wasn't just those two relationships that made me want to take my life. I also remembered something that happened to me when I was in the fifth grade. I was walking toward the lunchroom, and I saw my fifth-grade teacher. As I walked around the corner, I heard her say, "My students are so stupid."

Around that same age, I remembered being a very shy and quiet person. Because of my quiet demeanor, the kids at school used to beat me and call me gay. While I held the knife to my throat, all these thoughts played in my head as if I was being forced to watch a horror movie without a stop button. I didn't feel like I had any other option. I didn't believe I had any value. I was a Christian; I loved God, but I was sick and tired of the pain. I was tired of being hurt by people I once trusted. I was tired of being alive if I wasn't going to feel alive. I grazed the blade of the knife against my neck just to see what it might feel like if I were to cut myself wide open and bleed to death. I didn't want to live anymore, and I didn't know any other way to escape from the pain. I cried out to God, "I'm done with this life; just take me home."

CHAPTER 1

Renewing of the Mind

"Changing the way we think changes the way we live, which
will change the way we love, which changes the world."

"**Y**ou can't teach an old dog new tricks." While there is some truth to that statement, Joel Osteen once said, "I believe you *can*, but it depends on the dog." Romans 12:2 says, *Do not conform to the pattern of this world, but be transformed by the renewing of your mind. Then you will be able to test and approve what God's will is—his good, pleasing, and perfect will.* Renewing our minds is a choice we have to make every single day. Many of us continue to live in defeat because we don't believe that our situation will ever change. The truth is that when Jesus died on the cross and defeated death through His resurrection, prophetically, our situation had already changed. It's not the truth that changes us; it's us choosing to come to agreement with the truth that brings the change. When the way I think aligns with the way He thinks, heaven invades earth. Renewing the mind isn't just positive thinking—it's kingdom thinking.

Never Let Disappointment Set the Agenda

When I was in my early twenties, my friend Sandra and I were sending texts to each other, and we both became very engaged in the conversation. Then, all of a sudden, she said something to me in the text message that I never thought she would say. Because I didn't like what she said, I dropped an f-bomb in my reply and told her I never wanted to talk to her again. A few months after that, we reconciled but only because she was the bigger person by choosing to stay connected in our friendship. The reason I reacted that way when she sent me the message wasn't because of what she said. It was because I had been hurt by many friends in the past that had taken advantage of me. At that point in my life, I'd decided that no one was going to take advantage of me ever again. I was tired of feeling powerless in my relationships with people, so I decided that being controlling and manipulative was the solution to that problem.

What I hadn't realized was that by being controlling and manipulative, *I* was the one who was choosing to be powerless in my relationships with people. The reason I was acting this way was because I was afraid of being hurt, and hurt people hurt people. Pastor Danny Silk explained this perfectly when he said, "When we withhold love, anxiety fills the void, and the spirit of fear directs our behavior toward the offender." A relationship driven by fear isn't a relationship—it's a contract. In 1 John 4:18, it says, *There is no fear in love. But perfect love drives out fear, because fear has to do with punishment. The one who fears is not made perfect in love.* When we are filled with the love of God, we are no longer slaves to fear, but we are slaves to righteousness (Romans 6:18). It's natural for the carnal mind to revert to self-protection mode when someone has hurt us, but it's supernatural for the mind of Christ to release forgiveness toward our offender. God has given us the mind of Christ to choose love over fear with the people we are in covenant with (1 Corinthians 2:16).

A few years ago, I was honored to colead a program called Christ Life with my friend Roy Hamblin, a great man of God. Roy taught me that during conversations with people, I simply need to share things that I feel comfortable sharing rather than telling them that there are certain things I don't feel comfortable sharing. When I tell someone that I don't feel comfortable sharing something, a wall goes up in our relationship. I can know that there are certain things I don't want to share with someone, but it isn't *knowing* this that puts up the wall; it's *saying* it that instills fear into our connection. Although it's not always possible, our goal should be to focus on sharing what we want out of our relationships with people rather than focusing on sharing what we don't want.

Many of us have experienced emotional trauma from our bad experiences that has transformed the way we think. Being transformed by a bad experience gives us the false impression that the walls we've put up in our covenant relationships are what boundaries are supposed to look like. Walls keep everyone out, but boundaries draw the right people in. From what Roy taught me, I've learned that choosing to be vulnerable with people tears down the walls of fear and builds a foundation of trust. The more trust is developed in our relationship with someone, the more we will be willing to share our heart with that person.

When I realized I was scaring people away with my anger and bitterness, I knew I needed to change. The problem was that my focus didn't shift to "I want to be more like Jesus." It shifted to, "I don't want to be a bad person anymore." The problem with focusing on what I didn't want was that thinking this way didn't propel me into closer relationships with people. Just because we're in first gear doesn't mean we're going anywhere. If we truly want change in our relationships, we need to be vulnerable enough to apply the gas pedal and start going after intimacy with people the way Jesus did when He walked the earth. Changing the way we think changes the way we live, which will change the way we love, which changes the world.

It would be great if I were to say that I no longer have any struggles. It would be great for me to pretend that my life today is perfect, and I no longer experience pain or heartache. However, the truth is that I don't always have the right things to say; I still make bad decisions, and I still need to renew my mind on a daily basis. A person who never risks never falls, but with great risk comes great reward after rising from the fall.

Where there is no vision, the people perish: but he that keepeth the law, happy is he (Proverbs 29:18 KJV). We all need to have a vision for our lives in order to get back up after a disappointment; a vision gets you up every morning and keeps a smile on your face while people around you complain about their circumstances. God loves you where you are, but He loves you too much to leave you there. When we discover who our Daddy is and we realize that He is the Creator of this universe, we know that He has called us to make an impact in this world. When I wake up every day knowing that

I'm here with a divine purpose, it's easy to bounce back from a disappointment, but when I wake up thinking that God has predetermined the direction of my life and there's nothing I can do to change that, a disappointment could kill me. God works all things for the good of those who love Him (Romans 8:28), but God isn't in control of all things.

Bill Johnson, pastor of Bethel Church in Redding, California, once said, "Why would God raise something up to be His will that He empowers you to pray against?" The second half of 2 Peter 3:9 says, *Instead he is patient with you, not wanting anyone to perish, but everyone to come to repentance.*

Sickness isn't God's will; that's why we pray against it. Demonic oppression isn't God's will; that's why we love people until the demons jump out of them. God has given us control of the direction of our lives through the power of the Holy Spirit and the indwelling of Jesus Christ. Apart from Him I can do nothing, but when He lives in me, disappointment is just a speed bump on the road to my destiny. When I truly trust God with all of my heart, my bad experiences no longer have the authority to tell me the "truth" about God's will, but God's will tells me the truth about my bad experiences. Being transformed by the renewing of the mind isn't a "wham, bam, done!" type of process. This type of transformation is a daily choice for us to allow His love to continually change the way we think rather than letting broken people change the way we think. God doesn't put a desire in your heart, give you what you want, and then take it away from you to teach you a lesson. This is "the God Father," not to be confused with "God the Father." I believe that if we choose to continually be transformed by the renewing of our minds, God will restore the promises that have been stolen from us by the devil. The devil is the one who takes away, but when we believe in the power of the resurrection, God will give back more abundantly than we could ever imagine.

CHAPTER 2

The Innocence of a Child

*"When we learn to be like children, we realize that the
kingdom of heaven operates at a level of complexity that
only a child can understand."*

The Importance of Sonship

Growing up, I consistently felt like I wasn't good enough. I thought I wasn't good enough to graduate high school, I thought I wasn't good enough to be in a healthy relationship with a significant other, and I thought I wasn't good enough to be a father someday. I spent a lot of my teenage years and early twenties either dreaming about things that had no eternal significance or dreaming that I could be somebody else. I wanted to be someone people noticed, appreciated, and loved.

When I was in elementary school, I was very shy. I remember a kid named Andrew who would pick on me every once in a while. Every so often, he would punch me in the stomach in front of his friends, and they would all laugh at me. I didn't know how to defend myself, and I developed a bitterness and resentment toward him. I was bullied a lot from third grade through sixth. One day I decided to speak out about the abuse, and I shared it with a family friend who was a black belt in karate. Once I learned how to defend myself, going to school became easier for me, but I also developed a hardened heart toward other people's feelings. I wanted to protect myself from pain at all costs by living in isolation. Living in isolation was my way of guarding my heart, but it actually attracted the demonic realm into my life in a greater measure than I had ever experienced before. I may have learned how to defend myself against the people who were physically abusing me, but I didn't learn how to guard my heart.

It was experiences like these that accentuated many poor characteristics that were emerging in me: jealousy, outbursts of rage, passive aggression, and an orphan-victim mentality. Overall, I had a good childhood, and my parents loved me and raised me right, but I can remember always having visions and dreams about death and being alone. Many times I would feel like I wasn't wanted by anyone. While I was still in elementary school, I remember having a recurring dream in which I felt as if no one wanted me. In the dream, I was sitting in the backseat of a car while somebody I knew was driving. Then the car made a hard right turn, the left rear door opened, and I fell out of the car. I was hanging onto the door as it swung violently, while the car continued to accelerate. I screamed for help, but the people up front couldn't hear me. Eventually, my fingers slipped off the door, and I tumbled onto the ground and into a dark alley. I got up off the ground and watched the car race off into the darkness of the night. I had this same dream three times.

The bizarre thing is that not only did I have this same dream three times, but I also knew in both the second and third dream that

I had already had this experience before. In the second and third dream, I already knew what was going to happen, but I couldn't do anything to change the outcome, which made the experience more terrifying. This is how the devil wants us to think. He wants us to believe everything that will happen in our lives is already predestined. The enemy wants us to think that our destiny is controlled by fate, but the truth is that our fate starts and ends with the way we think. In his book *Spirit Wars*, Pastor Kris Vallotton said, "When we fill our minds with negative predictions or allow our thoughts to manipulate us into thinking about all the possible destructive outcomes of our mission, we invite fear to paralyze our progress; but when we press past the intimidation of demonic spirits and commit even more resolutely to finishing our divine assignments, we torment the tormentors and they lose their confidence."

Aside from being bullied, I was also verbally abused throughout elementary school because of my quiet demeanor. Many kids would call me gay because I was shy. I knew I wasn't gay, because I had a crush on one of the girls in my class, until one day I thought I was. I had heard "You're gay" so many times that I developed an attraction to one of my male friends in class. It was only a split-second thought, but shame and guilt plagued my mind afterward. "How could I be gay?" I thought to myself. "If that's what everyone keeps telling me, then maybe I *am* gay." I told God that I would never tell anyone about that thought. I told God that I would take that thought to the grave with me. It wasn't until about fifteen years later that I finally decided to be transparent with people about that experience. Never again have I had a homosexual thought since that day. As the years went on, I processed this experience with both the Holy Spirit and people I trusted, and I learned that children build their identity from either the people or family that surrounds them.

Since I've had this experience, I've developed a bigger heart toward the gay community. If homosexuals don't encounter the source of love through Christians, they will continue to try and find love in other places. Children will believe almost anything they're told. If they're taught God's truth, then they'll live by that truth. But if they're taught lies, then they'll live by those lies unless they receive inner healing. *Start children off on the way they should go, and even when they are old they will not turn from it* (Proverbs 22:6).

Being Childlike

And he said: "Truly I tell you, unless you change and become like little children, you will never enter the kingdom of heaven" (Matthew 18:3). As a child, I can remember enjoying all of the things most children enjoyed in American culture during that time—Mario Bros., the Power Rangers, birthday parties—but most importantly, I enjoyed spending time with friends and family. When I was a young kid, I remember spending time with my brothers, David and J. J., and my sisters, Jessica and Esme. I specifically remember spending a lot of time with them playing games late into the night. Though I remember the games we played were a lot of fun, the memories I really hold on to are the ones in which we just spent time together without a care in the world. Despite the bad experiences I had growing up, one of the best parts about being a child that I can remember was not being consumed and burdened by responsibilities; I believe this is partially what Jesus meant when He told us to become like children. Children are able to receive freely without analyzing everything. Many times I feel nostalgic when I think back to the good times I spent with my blood-related brothers and sisters. One of the problems with many adults is that we fall into this mentality that everything in life is a responsibility.

As adults, many of us think, "I have to go to work; otherwise, I won't have a house to live in," or "I can't have another child, because that would be another financial burden," and so on. I believe sometimes we confuse being childlike with being childish. God wants us to think like children, not behave like them. In order to be childlike, we need to change the way we think. If I view everything I do in life as a responsibility, I will never truly live—I will merely exist. Sometimes, when I drive by a graveyard and look at all the graves, I think to myself, "I wonder if all of those people lived up to their God-given potential? I wonder if one of them would have created the cure for cancer or birthed the next great revival. I wonder how many of their hopes and dreams died long before they passed away." If I had the choice between living a life where I had to die to make an impact that rippled into the next generation or to live a life that was safe and started and ended with me, I would choose the former of the two. *For to me, to live is Christ and to die is gain* (Philippians 1:21). Jesus didn't die on the cross so that we would die but so that we would live life in abundance. Pastor Bill Johnson once said, "Jesus got what we deserved so that He could give us what He deserved."

Game Changers: JC Sacramento Children's Ministry
At Jesus Culture church in Sacramento, I've had the opportunity to serve on the children's ministry team, and I am truly blessed to

have been part of such an amazing ministry. I haven't always been a kid person; I was the type of guy who used to stand around like a piece of cardboard while children would run around me playing and screaming like a bunch of wild monkeys. Children don't have boundaries, they don't have expectations, and they don't hold grudges—they just love. Children have an advantage over adults, as far as receiving God's love is concerned; they don't have bad experiences that would influence a definition of love that attracts evil spirits. I believe this is one of the reasons Jesus said that we need to be like children to see the kingdom—children will believe just about anything they're told. When they're told the truth about who God is and what love looks like, it positions them to start and steward a revival compelled by love that will change the world.

At Game Changers, I worked wherever help was needed. The first thing we did while I was serving at Game Changers was to ask the children to gather in a circle so they can each share something really cool about themselves. This is a great way to break the ice for some of the shyer children. One of the things I came to realize quickly is that in a crowd of obedient children, there's always going to be the ones that just want to break the rules. One of the things I've learned from Danny Silk is that we love people for who they are, but we don't allow their bad behavior to thrive in our relationship with them. One of the things we practice at Jesus Culture church is to call people into who they are rather than focus on their bad behavior. When we say things to the children such as, "You're too awesome to be acting like that," it separates the way a child behaves from the person God called them to be. Christianity is not a behavioral rehab program that focuses on making bad people good; it's a relationship with a good Father whose love compels us to go from dead to alive.

I believe it's this type of mentality that makes Game Changers such a powerful ministry. We empower the children to dream. When children learn at an early age that they're not going to be rewarded by having a bad attitude, it prepares them to steward a revival that never ends. God will never give us more than we can handle, but if we don't steward what He gives us, we'll never be able to handle any more. Love is the foundation of relationships, relationships are the foundation of a healthy culture, and a healthy culture is the foundation of revival. At Game Changers, we give the children a snack time and a story time, and then, finally, we all gather for a corporate ministry time. During ministry time, we do worship first, and then we get into the Word. One of the things I noticed, particularly through the worship time, is that the children are hungry—they're hungry for a relationship. God created us for love, and I believe that children's ministry is one of the most powerful ways for us to equip the next generation with the spiritual tools they need to change the world through the supernatural power of love.

One of the things that I still cannot wrap my mind around is the fact that children don't have expectations. There are a few instances while serving at Game Changers where all I needed to do was start making funny faces with the kids, and all of a sudden they were my best friends. The level of intimacy that children are able to develop with one another is astounding. Sometimes I stop and think to myself, "Why am I not I as transparent, vulnerable, and straightforward as these children? Why do I need to be careful with certain people to avoid offending them, and why do some people feel they need to be careful so they don't offend me?" Yikes! Keeping the right attitude in a situation that is not in my favor is like rubbing sandpaper on a rusted classic car. It may hurt now, but if we keep the right attitude, it will reveal a masterpiece later. Many of us are rusted cars who get offended with anyone and everyone that doesn't agree with us.

Since I'm a car guy, the best way for me to explain this would be by using a car analogy. As a rusted car, we begin to think that the outside world is the problem, so we isolate ourselves in our garages while we wait for the perfect day to share our hearts with people. Of course, the perfect day never comes. A classic car will never be new again, but if that car has been sanded of all imperfections, it can be "like new" again. This is what I believe Jesus meant when He told us to be "like" children. Sometimes I wish I could protect every child from ever having a bad experience. Sometimes I wish I could keep them in a bubble so that they don't need to experience the type of pain I've experienced in my relationships with people. As much as I would like to do that, however, I've learned that preventing children from having their own experiences is actually just as dangerous as letting them do whatever they want.

Love doesn't give people the freedom to do whatever they want to us, but it gives people the strength to do whatever is right (Ephesians 3:16). I believe that as we continue to learn from little children and be childlike, we will also live like them. We will live free from fear, debt, anger, bitterness, sexual immorality, and judgment. And most importantly, in my opinion, we'll be free from living in isolation.

When we learn to be like children, we realize that the kingdom of heaven operates at a level of complexity that only a child can understand. In the natural world, we need to grow up, but in a spiritual sense, we need to grow down. In the natural world, we build skyscrapers, we lead nations, we invest, we start businesses, and we build fame and fortune. But for many of us, we don't know how to love. By learning how to love, we will learn how to live. *Therefore, whoever takes the lowly position of this child is the greatest in the kingdom of heaven* (Matthew 18:4). Love looks like the heart of a child, and when we have the heart of a child, that's when heaven comes down and changes the world.

CHAPTER 3

Perfectly Broken

"To love is to be vulnerable, to heal is to be intentional,
and to love again is transformational."

Knocking on Death's Door

It was some years back when I felt so close to death that I could almost taste it. I remember it like it was yesterday. It was a warm summer night. A friend's family invited me over to their house for dinner. When I arrived at their house, I immediately recognized a bunch of friends from church. But only one of them caught my attention—Kendra. At that time, I was interested in pursuing Kendra. I had expressed my feelings to her, but she told me that she needed some time to think about that. The uncertainty left me with all types of tormenting thoughts. After about ten minutes or so, my friend Justin yelled out, "All right, guys—food's ready! Let's say a prayer and dig in!" At that moment, all of us found a seat and prepared for the awesome meal.

About thirty minutes into our meal, Kendra's phone rang. Surprised, she said to everyone, "I'm so sorry. I totally forgot to put my phone on vibrate!" Once she quickly finished cleaning her hands, she ran to the back porch, slid open the screen door, and answered her phone.

In the meantime, after my friends and I had finished our meal, my friend Justin said, "Now who's ready for dessert?" Everyone looked at each other and chuckled nervously. Noticing the look on everyone's face, Justin said, "Come on guys! I know you still have room for some white-chocolate cookies mixed with caramel and ice cream!"

I looked at everyone and said, "I'll make room for that!" After everyone was served dessert, I realized that I could hear Kendra's conversation with her friend through the back patio screen door. Not wanting to eavesdrop, I tried to ignore it until I heard her say something that caught my attention.

Kendra said, "Yeah, so there's this guy I met recently. I really like him a lot. He's really old-fashioned, and he even bought me flowers!" After Kendra said that, I knew she wasn't talking about me. At that moment, it seemed like the whole world slowed down. That night, it rained heavily and lightning lit up the dark sky, which rarely happened. Right then I was reminded of a very similar situation that took place only one year prior to this experience. It was an extremely frightening moment of déjà vu:

It was Sunday morning. I was lying in bed, but I hadn't slept all night because I was plagued with tormenting thoughts about a woman named Veronica. Veronica and I had only been dating for about a month, but it seemed like we'd known each other much longer. Everything seemed to be going well between us until about two days before. I remembered having lunch with a few friends, and all of a sudden Veronica's friend Rebecca said something that shocked me. Veronica didn't eat lunch with us that day, so Rebecca said, "Hey, guys! So guess what? Veronica might be dating Tim! She told me all about him last night, and I think they'd make a cute couple!" After Rebecca said that, it seemed like everything was moving in slow motion. I continued to laugh and smile with everyone so I didn't draw attention to myself, but inside, I was in a world of pain. While all of these thoughts were going through my head that Sunday morning, I knew I had to do something, so I called Veronica. "Hey, Ernesto!" Veronica said.

"Hey! How are you?" I asked.

"I'm good. I'm just making breakfast and cleaning things up around the house. What's up?"

Nervously I said, "There's some stuff we need to talk about. Are you free to meet up later this morning?"

"Is everything OK? I mean, I do have plans today, but if it's serious, I can meet with you later this morning."

"I'm sorry about that, but it is really important. Are you able to meet at the coffee shop we always go to?"

"Sure," she said. "I'll see you there in a bit."

When both of us arrived at the coffee shop, Veronica got out of her car and walked up to me with a confused look on her face; she knew something was wrong. I said, "Let's sit here if that sounds good to you."

"OK."

After we both sat down in the outdoor patio section of the coffee shop, she looked at me and said, "What's going on?"

Several seconds later, I said, "Are you dating Tim?"

Veronica's demeanor changed. She lowered her head and looked at the ground as if she were filled with guilt and shame. She finally replied, "I'm not dating Tim. Where did you hear that?"

"I heard it from your best friend, Rebecca, the other day. Is that true?"

Veronica, refusing to look at me, said, "Tim and I are not dating. About a month ago, Tim told me that he was interested in pursuing me. I told him that I wasn't ready for a relationship and that I needed to take time to think about it."

Shocked, I said, "You needed to take time to think about it? Does that mean that you don't think there's anything going on between you and me?"

She seemed embarrassed. "No! That's not it. I'm not interested in him in that way."

I was confused. "If you weren't interested in him in that way, then why didn't you just tell him you weren't interested?"

Veronica started to shiver, and I could see her eyes watering. "I knew all of this wasn't going to work."

I waited for several seconds. I took a deep breath and said, "Look, if you want to date Tim, you can date Tim. He's a great guy, and I don't have anything bad to say about him. But if that's the decision you make, then we cannot continue to see each other anymore."

Tears streamed down her face. "I don't wanna date Tim! You know, the truth about all of this is that I don't want to date you either. I just wanna be your friend—that's it."

"No, that's not true. You do want us to date, but you're just afraid."

With tears streaming down her face, she looked me in the eyes. "I'm scared."

"You don't have to be scared. Everything is going to be all right. The reason I brought this up is because I want us to be honest with each other about our relationship."

She wiped her tears, looked at me, and said, "Does this mean we're not going to go to the beach together later this summer?"

"Of course, we're still going to the beach together; that hasn't changed. Why don't we take a couple of days to process what just happened between us, and on Tuesday, we'll talk more about that. Does that sound good?"

Veronica smiled. "That sounds good. Actually, you know what? I've got to go now. I still need to finish making breakfast and clean things up around the house. Well, I'll see you later." She got up and started walking back to her car.

"I can't get a hug before you leave?" I asked. She stopped and we both wrapped our arms around one another. It was the longest I had ever hugged Veronica. After that, we said our good-byes. She slowly walked back to her car, dragging her feet, her head hung low. A couple of days later, on Tuesday, I couldn't wait to talk to her. I was looking forward to planning our date to the beach.

When Tuesday evening came, I called her, but she didn't answer the phone, so I left a message. After a few hours passed, I knew something was wrong. I called her again, but she didn't answer the phone. I decided not to leave another message—one was enough. She never did return my phone call. That Sunday morning when Veronica walked away from me, with tears in her eyes and her head hung low, was the last time I ever heard from or saw her again.

My memory of the incident with Veronica was circling though my head when I overheard Kendra tell her friend that she was dating another guy; I had gone through this before. That dark and stormy night, I decided not to confront Kendra about the issue because I didn't want to risk losing her as a friend. Later that night, my emotions were so out of control that I didn't know what to do with myself. I paced around my room for about an hour or so while trying to think about something pleasant. To say that my heart had been broken is an understatement; it felt like someone had reached into my chest, grabbed my heart, and wrung it so tightly that it sucked me dry of all possible life and hope.

When I tried to breathe, I could feel a tight pain in my chest so intense that I felt claustrophobic. The experience was so traumatic that I wasn't quite sure how to react to it. I didn't get angry, and I didn't cry, because I already knew reacting that way in the past had never changed anything. I was numb to my emotions. For about an hour or so, my facial expression didn't change. Never in my entire life had I ever experienced this level of pain. It seemed like every moment of rejection that I'd ever experienced in my entire life was brought to the forefront of my memory bank: Kendra rejecting me for another guy, Veronica rejecting me for Tim, my elementary school teacher saying, "My students are so stupid," the kids at school calling me gay, and so on. I was so overwhelmed with all of these tormenting thoughts that I decided to go into my kitchen, grab a knife, and kill myself. Looking back at this situation, I realized I had probably had a nervous breakdown. I was thinking back to all of the times that I had thought about killing myself. I had visions and dreams about death during very dark moments of my life. I was tired of experiencing pain, I was tired of being disappointed, and I was tired of feeling like I was simply getting older but not going anywhere significant in my life. I knew the Bible inside and out, I could prophesy over people all day long and get all the words right, I could pray for healing and see the sick healed, but I didn't know my identity in Christ or how to receive love.

When I stepped into the kitchen, I grabbed a large knife from the drawer and held it to my throat. I grazed the blade of the knife on my neck just to get an idea of what it might feel like if I were to cut my neck open and bleed to death. As I held the knife I prayed, "God, I'm done with disappointment. I'm done with pain. I'm done with this place. Please take me home." Even at that moment, I was still emotionless. I don't even think I knew how to feel anymore. I held the knife for a couple of minutes, and then I heard God speak. He said, *Son, if you really want to die, then die for a cause. Don't die for nothing.* It was at that moment that everything changed for me. I put the knife away, and then I began to feel. As soon as I knew what to do with my emotions, tears started streaming down my face. I cried so hard that I got a headache, but that didn't stop the tears from flowing. I knew God wasn't finished with me yet. I don't think I slept at all that night, even though I tried. I spent the rest of the night watching Heidi Baker teachings about the love of God. It was that night I realized that, for all the years I'd been alive, I'd had it all wrong.

I am not here to build an empire for myself. I'm not here to work at the perfect job, live in the perfect house, have the perfect family, or live the perfect life, because it's all a perfect lie. I'm here to love and to be loved. I feel like this is the point in my life where

I was just beginning to understand the depths of God's love. To love is to be vulnerable, to heal is to be intentional, and to love again is transformational. True love always trusts, it always hopes, it always perseveres, and it never fails. Love is more than a feeling; love is a person who gave His life so that we would be alive and thrive in our relationships with people. One of the biggest reasons I believe this traumatic situation took place in my life is because I didn't know how to guard my heart. *Above all else, guard your heart, for everything you do flows from it* (Proverbs 4:23). Guarding my heart doesn't mean I punish people for hurting me; it means I'm vulnerable enough to share what hurts my heart so that we can focus on growing together in love.

Shutting down and giving people the silent treatment has nothing to do with love. I can say with confidence that I have reconciled, both directly and indirectly, with everyone from my past that has caused me pain. For me, forgiveness is not optional; it's a way of life. I'm always growing in the love of God. But I will say that I've gotten to the point at which, as long as I can help it, I refuse to lose any more friends regardless of who was wronged. Relationships aren't about who's right and who's wrong. They're about building love and intimacy with people and keeping that as the focus. If there's something I can do to protect, nurture, and develop a relationship I have with someone, I will do everything in my power to do so, even if I don't agree with the other person. Pastor Danny Silk once said, "Free people are going to tell you the truth, and they are going to make mistakes; this will not only test the relationship, but it will test the state of your heart." I believe that sometimes it's in the most broken and vulnerable places in our lives that we can encounter God at His greatest. One of the best places to be is in a position where we're fully postured, fully submitted, and totally desperate for an encounter with the very heartbeat of God.

Carry Your Cross

Then Jesus said to his disciples, "Whoever wants to be my disciple must deny themselves and take up their cross and follow me. For whoever wants to save their life will lose it, but whoever loses their life for me will find it" (Matthew 16:24–25). I believe this verse applies to so many areas of our lives. One of the most difficult things to deal with in the body of Christ is the spirit of offense. There are a couple of reasons the spirit of offense can happen. We can become offended when we pray for something to happen, knowing it aligns with the will of God, yet the outcome is negative without any explanation. Another reason we can become offended is when someone we honor disagrees with something we are passionate about. I believe there is a direct connection between the renewing of the mind and carrying your cross. The renewing of the mind is a very painful process. Most of us would rather run away from pain than face it and let Jesus renew our minds through the process.

A large part of renewing the mind is learning how to carry our cross full of pain through the desert into our promised land flowing with milk and honey. Many of us would rather give up, run from our pain, and try to enter into the Promised Land effortlessly. When we refuse to carry our cross, we become a people who are satisfied with the idea of bringing heaven to earth, but we have no authority to release heaven to the earth because of unaddressed disappointment and fear. The disappointment wars against our mandate to bring His kingdom to earth because it entertains thoughts that partner with the spirit of fear. Scripture tells us that the kingdom of heaven is within us (Luke 17:21 KJV), but when we have fear rooted in us, it's like a basket has covered the light of heaven that we carry. Jesus died on the cross to do more than just get us into heaven—He did it to bring the reality of heaven into us.

One of the most complex questions believers ask themselves is why God allows death and sickness in the world. We know it's not God's will that any should perish (2 Peter 3:9), but many people die every day, even after others have prayed for them. As of this writing, I had a friend pass away from a long battle with brain cancer. I have always heard stories of other people losing their loved ones to cancer, but this one hit closer to home than I was comfortable with. I remember the first time I met my friend Jeff at Bethel Church. I was in the Great Room, worshipping with many other passionate worshipers. The Lord prompted me to give him a prophetic word, and when I did, he burst into tears. After I finished praying for him, he explained why he was crying. Some years prior, God had healed him of brain cancer, but the cancer came back. After Jeff said that, a large group of us feverishly commanded the brain tumor to disappear permanently in the name of Jesus.

After we finished praying for Jeff, I continued to talk with him for a while. Jeff told me about his dreams, his family, his hobbies, and his passion for Jesus. I had known Jeff for about three and a half years, and during the last year of his life, he progressively got worse rather quickly. Many people, including myself, continued to pray for him relentlessly, believing and trusting God for a supernatural miracle. Sadly, despite all the prayers, Jeff eventually went to be with the Lord. This experience did move me, but my foundation wasn't shaken. I have seen God open blind eyes, fix deaf ears, and grow out people's legs that weren't the same length as their other leg, so I knew that God had the ability to remove the brain tumor from Jeff. But it didn't happen. As of this writing, I've been going through a few stages of grief with Jeff. I've been sad, then angry, and then frustrated. But at the end of the day, this experience has made me even more passionate about seeing God bring healing and restoration to people.

While I still don't have an answer as to why Jeff wasn't healed, I know that God is always good. What I believe "carry your cross" means in this particular situation is to not allow this bad experience to change the way I think about who God is and what He is capable of. Sometimes it hurts more to believe that God is good during a time of tragedy than it is to believe He did it to teach us a lesson. "Carry your cross" doesn't mean that God gives us mysterious illnesses to humble us. It means we continue to believe that God is good when it feels like He's not. The way I view "carrying my cross" is that the longer I righteously suffer for love (1 Corinthians 13:4 KJV), the stronger my spiritual muscles become. Different translations of the Bible say that love is patient, but most of us would agree that being patient can be very painful. I believe the greatest reward for carrying our cross is not just to experience life in abundance, but also to encounter His love in abundance.

True love never fails, not because fate has determined for it to be that way, but because sons and daughters of God choose for it to be that way. We must learn to carry our cross beyond the death of a loved one, beyond a divorce, beyond a suicide, beyond a mental illness, and beyond the repressed memories of those who have treated us poorly. We carry our crosses, because regardless of what we've experienced in the past, we want to believe for the dead to rise, for a marriage to be restored, for loneliness to be recompensed, and for mental illness to be healed. In order for love to never fail, we must never give up on people, because Jesus never gives up on us. There's a saying: "If you don't live for something, you'll die for nothing." I believe this means we need to live with a divine perspective. We are not here to merely go to work, pay taxes, and have a better-looking car than the Joneses. We're called to love people so radically that even if we disagree with them, we will pursue those relationships no matter the cost.

What I'm *not* trying to say when I talk about carrying your cross is that you need to put up with abusive people in your relationships. People who are abusive, whether it's verbally or physically, are so gripped with fear and insecurity that they feel controlling other people is the best way to guard their heart from being hurt again. We must love these people and accept them for who we know they *really* are, but we must also understand that love sets boundaries and isn't afraid to correct bad behavior. *Because the LORD disciplines those he loves, as a father the son he delights in* (Proverbs 3:12). I am not a professional counselor, so the advice that I give can only help so many people because every situation looks different.

One great way to discipline people who are abusive is to communicate with them how the way they act hurts our heart. Women are naturally better at doing this than men, but I believe that God is raising a generation of men who know how to love people radically. One of the reasons we don't want to be vulnerable enough to share our heart with an angry person is because that person has already introduced us to a spirit of fear. For many of us, when fear is introduced in our relationship with someone, the human desire is to overpower the other person with words that are more painful than the ones spoken to us. When this happens, both people end up in a relationship where being right is the goal. A child of God understands that "turn the other cheek" doesn't mean that I give people permission to take advantage of me but that my desire to demonstrate sacrificial love is greater than my desire to defend what I think I deserve.

I believe there is a powerful biblical perspective when it comes to dealing with people who are abusive. Matthew 18:15–17 says*: If your brother or sister sins, go and point out their fault, just between the two of you. If they listen to you, you have won them over. But if they will not listen, take one or two others along, so that every matter may be established by the testimony of two or three witnesses. If they still refuse to listen, tell it to the church; and if they refuse to listen even to the church, treat them as you would a pagan or a tax collector.* Most of us would like to create an ultimatum the first time someone sins against us. We tend to say things such as, "I can't believe you did that! If you ever do that again, I'm never going to talk to you again!" Many people choose to live in isolation for this very reason. Love doesn't exist in a relationship in which the other person is afraid to hurt my feelings because I might threaten the relationship. When a brother or sister sins against me, as it says in Scripture, my number-one goal is to bring up the issue with that person before even thinking about telling anyone else.

Some years ago, a friend and I used to talk all the time, almost every day. Then one day, I called my friend and she didn't answer the phone. I was a little frustrated with her, but I figured she was probably busy. Over the next two or three days, I continued to call my friend, and she still didn't answer the phone. I became so angry with her that I decided to delete her phone number, delete her from all of my social-media networks, and never talk to her again. Because social media is the ultimate form of revelation when it comes to communicating our hearts with those we love (I'm totally joking, of course), I believed that ignoring her and disconnecting with her was the best way to show her that I wasn't going to be taken advantage of.

I can't even believe that I used to think that way. It makes me sick to my stomach to even think about how many friends I lost by having that type of mentality. Now, don't get me wrong—what my friend did *was* very hurtful, but I didn't know how to communicate that with her in a healthy way. The best decision in a situation like that would have been for me to share how the lack of communication was hurting our relationship. The reason we open our hearts with people by revealing to them how much their actions are hurting us isn't to threaten our connection with them. It's so that we will use the supernatural power of communication to strengthen our relationship. Sometimes when we reveal our heart, in love, to an immature person, this will actually destroy the connection. Other people might not be currently capable of intimacy to the same degree that we are. Whatever the outcome, we must not become offended when people disconnect from us, because Jesus is always reaching His hand out to us.

Again, every situation is different, and one size doesn't fit all. Staying connected with people who may not want anything to do with us will look different for everyone. Whatever the scenario may be, the focus is always to stay connected at a level of intimacy the other person is capable of receiving love. Once in a great while, people we are in covenant with will stop calling us, stop talking to us, or move away without any explanation. In cases like these, we must fight the temptation to jump to a conclusion as to why that happened if we've already done our part by trying to reconnect. Should that person decide one day to reconnect with us, we must also avoid the temptation to say things such as, "You've had your chance, and now it's over" or "I told you to listen to me, but now it's too late for you to apologize."

Carrying your cross means being willing to take people, who genuinely repent, back with open arms and let them know how much we've missed them. We don't need to remind them of all the times they've hurt us, because love doesn't keep a record of wrongs (1 Corinthians 13:5). We don't even need to tell them how hurt we were that they disappeared from our lives without an explanation; all we need to do is accept them, love them, and welcome them back home. One of the best examples in Scripture of how to carry our cross and persevere with love is the story of the prodigal son.

Jesus continued: There was a man who had two sons. The younger one said to his father, "Father, give me my share of the estate." So he divided his property between them. Not long after that, the younger son got together all he had, set off for a distant country and there squandered his wealth in wild living. After he had spent everything, there was a severe famine in that whole country, and he began to be in need. So he went and hired himself out to a citizen of that country, who sent him to his fields to feed pigs. He longed to fill his stomach with the pods that the pigs were eating, but no one gave him anything. When he came to his senses, he said, "How many of my father's hired servants have food to spare, and here I am starving to death! I will set out and go back to my father and say to him: 'Father, I have sinned against heaven and against you. I am no longer worthy to be called your son; make me like one of your hired servants.'" So he got up and went to his father. But while he was still a long way off, his father saw him and was filled with compassion for him; he ran to his son, threw his arms around him and kissed him. The son said to him, "Father, I have sinned against heaven and against you. I am no longer worthy to be called your son."

But the father said to his servants, "Quick! Bring the best robe and put it on him. Put a ring on his finger and sandals on his feet. Bring the fattened calf and kill it. Let's have a feast and celebrate. For this son of mine was dead and is alive again; he was lost and is found." So they began to celebrate (Luke 15:11–24).

There are many times in our relationships that we are the ones who are immature and need to be corrected. *Whoever loves discipline loves knowledge, but whoever hates correction is stupid* (Proverbs 12:1). That's an extreme statement, but He's an extreme God who's passionate about us living in both breakthrough and victory.

There was a time when I was serving on the leadership team at Epic Life young adults group in Sacramento, California. Eric Waterbury, one of my lead pastors, met with me to discuss something really important. He told me that I had developed an independent mind-set that was driven by self-promotion. It hit me like a ton of bricks. I never saw myself as being arrogant enough to promote myself, but arrogance usually isn't something that develops overnight. The next thing he said to me was so powerful that it blew me away. He said, "Ernesto, the reason I'm telling you this is because I want you to fully step into the destiny that God has planned for you." That was a tough pill to swallow, but I knew that if I was ever going to gain any authority in the kingdom, I had to learn how to grow spiritually through the process of correction. God confirmed what Eric said shortly after, when I drove up to Bethel Church in Redding, California. Kris Vallotton preached about the dangers of self-promotion slipping into the church among leaders.

As I processed all of this, God revealed something to me. I realized that I had been taking advice from secular sources about how to be successful. While I don't believe there's anything wrong with taking advice from secular sources, we do need to be careful with who we allow to speak into the deepest crevices of our heart. I was told that I had to promote myself to get people to recognize me. Pastor Bill Johnson once said, "Whatever you gain through self-promotion you'll have to sustain through self-promotion. When our promotion comes from God, He sustains it." Along with the great wisdom my parents have imparted through the years, Eric Waterbury has played a major role in my spiritual growth. I'm very grateful to have him in my life to guide me into my destiny. I don't believe in tough love, but I believe in agape love, which is the nature of God. True love is unconditional, but it does set boundaries. It sets boundaries to protect the relationship from the fiery arrows of fear, insecurity, passive-aggressive behavior, control, and manipulation, to name a few.

Many of these poor character traits keep us circling around in the desert for forty years. Essentially, we tie God's hands behind His back when we continue to operate as orphans in our covenant relationships with people instead of as sons and daughters of the King. One of the ways I carry my cross daily is by reading my mission statement that I have framed on the wall in my room. It says, "Help others live their dreams, love people, be fearless, love radically, travel often, seek counsel, serve others, stay fit, be quick to forgive (myself), take risks, forgive others, be humble, be vulnerable, love Jesus, be generous, live a powerful life, never give up, change the world."

CHAPTER 4

Shining in Darkness

*"As essential as it is to demonstrate the power of God on
earth, we become powerless when we mirror His power
without mirroring His character."*

You Are the Light of the World

In my teenage years, I didn't know my identity in Christ. I
went through different stages, wanting to be a carpenter, a
master mechanic, a rapper, and so on. It was safe to say that I was
having an identity crisis. I knew that I was a Christian, but I always
thought that being a Christian started and ended with church on
Sunday and reading the Bible before bedtime. To think that I could
actually make a difference in the world never dawned on me.
If all of us knew who we were in Christ, we would all be doing
something powerful with our lives and letting our light shine in
the darkest places of the earth. In America, we have many distractions that hide our light such as music, movies, smartphones, video
games, the Internet, social media, television, and so on.

These sources often paint a picture of what love looks like,
and it's almost always a distorted perspective. I believe that

entertainment is a basket that covers our light, and this is a big thing that makes us ineffective in our God-given assignment. *No one lights a lamp and puts it in a place where it will be hidden, or under a bowl. Instead they put it on its stand, so that those who come in may see the light* (Luke 11:33). Entertainment isn't wrong in itself, but when it consumes our minds, we become transformed by a delusional version of reality that we can never get enough of. Being excessively entertained turns a desire into a fantasy and hope into a fairy tale based on half-truths and whole lies. We live in a country and generation in which we have 100 percent access to entertainment right at our fingertips. It's more difficult for us to be a light to the world when the tree of knowledge is within arm's reach. It's harder, but not impossible, to let the light of Jesus shine through us.

One encounter can change everything. A few years ago, a revivalist by the name of Brian Orme laid hands on me. I felt drunk in the Spirit (Ephesians 5:18). That moment may have not been my turning point, but it did change my theology about who God is and why I'm here. As a light to the world, our goal isn't to destroy darkness. Our goal is to turn darkness into light. The difference between the two is that when we focus on destroying darkness, we destroy people's hearts in the process. But when we focus on turning darkness into light, we are letting the power of love reveal the God-given identity of those living in darkness.

Several years ago, I was working at an automotive-repair shop with a verbally abusive manager. His name was Derek, and he would cuss me out and yell at me whenever I made a mistake. He used fear and manipulation to get all of us to do whatever he wanted. At that point in my life, I didn't know who I was in Christ. I thought that love meant that it was OK for people to treat me however they wanted and that I just had to be strong and take it. Since all of the other associates felt the same way I did, the abuse went on for years. Once in a while, we tried to report him for the abuse, but because the main store managers knew Derek on a personal level, they protected his position by disregarding our reports. Derek was a man with a very bad temper. I can remember how he would punch holes in the walls, throw chairs around his office, flip over tire machines in the shop, and throw things at people.

One day Derek and I had a confrontation about something that I wasn't doing right. I was very angry with him, and he knew that, so he asked me to follow him into the shop. I thought that Derek wanted to yell at me like he always did, so I followed him filled with anger yet afraid at the same time. Once we got to the shop, he turned around and said, "You want to hit me, don't you?" I looked at him with rage burning inside of me. Seeing the anger in my eyes, Derek said, "Go ahead—give me your best shot!" He held both of his hands out in an aggressive stance, as if he were ready to fight.

I had so much anger burning inside of me that I wanted to strangle him. He continued to stare at me with a sadistic smile on his face. I clenched my fists so tightly that I became afraid of what I was capable of. Crazy thoughts went through my head: "I think I'm about to go to jail right now, because this guy is going to get his face pounded!" Derek stood in that position for about ten to fifteen seconds, but it felt like an eternity.

Finally he said to me, "You can't hit me, because you're just a baby." He walked away. I never reported that to anyone because I was afraid Derek had the power to fire me. I had bought into the lie that someone had the ability to control me. Eventually he got fired, but the reason I share this story is because after I quit that job, I ran into a former employee that used to work for the same company. The former employee, Tom, told me that I was a very good person to be able to keep the right attitude in the middle of the abuse I went through. Even though Tom is older than me, he went so far as to say that he looked up to me for my integrity and that I was a great example in such a dark situation. For some reason I never thought of myself that way. I had repressed this entire experience. Until Tom told me that, I had never really considered the situation that bad.

If I had known everything I know now about who I am in Christ, I would never have allowed that type of abuse to continue for as long as it did. But there are a lot of people who feel just as powerless about making a difference as I did in that situation. Without realizing it, I was a light in that situation. To this day, there are still people who worked for that company that have told me how encouraged they were by my patience in that situation. I didn't think that I was making a difference, but I was. I wouldn't recommend handling an abusive relationship the way I did at that time, being as ignorant as I was. But God will use all things for good if we keep the right attitude. When we do the best with what we know, God not only increases our knowledge, but He also delivers us from darkness and uses our deliverance as a testimony to heal others that are still living in darkness.

Honoring Authorities

God equips us, promotes us, and sends us out to make a difference when we learn to keep the right attitude during dark seasons. King

Saul, from Scripture, chased David around for many years. But even when God gave David an opportunity to kill King Saul, David said, *The Lord forbid that I should do such a thing to my master, the Lord's anointed, or lay my hand on him; for he is the anointed of the Lord* (see 1 Samuel 24:6). While I'm thankful to God that I have never experienced this type of extreme ministry abuse, this passage blows my mind because it teaches us that character matters if we want to make a difference. As essential as it is to demonstrate the power of God on earth (see Romans 15:19), we become powerless when we mirror His power without mirroring His character. It is impossible to separate the power of God from the love of God because they're both part of His divine nature. What amazed me most about the story of David and King Saul is that David continued to persevere, regardless of his bad experiences, to believe that God was going to use him as a light to the world by honoring King Saul. Finally, after many years of David enduring the abuse of King Saul, the story ends with God promoting David to become king.

I have friends who have shared with me that certain church leaders are abusing their authority. When this happens, first I empathize with them, but then I ask them what they're going to do about it. Many times people are thrown off guard when I ask them this question, because they think I wasn't listening to their story. They think I'm going to sympathize with them, but I would rather empathize with them; they are not the same. Having *empathy* means understanding and sharing others' feelings, but having *sympathy* means feeling sorry for someone. People want to be understood, and I believe the best way to understand people is to empathize with them when they are struggling. Sympathy may look like empathy on the surface, but sympathizing with people too much can lead to a codependent relationship in which one person depends on the other person to survive. People with a victim mentality are always looking for someone to sympathize with them because they refuse to take control of their lives. When I have the love of God abiding within me, its fruits will reveal that the only person who has authority to control me, is me (Galatians 5:22–23).

People with a victim mentality cannot be a light to the world if they're always running away from darkness. One of the best ways to help this type of people is to teach them that they can actually do something about their circumstances, while at the same time empathizing with them about their painful experiences. Sympathy usually teaches people that their identity derives from their pain, but empathy teaches people how to thrive *because* of their pain. When people who have been abused by authoritative figures learn how to thrive because of their pain, they'll carry a new level of authority to shine their light to a world full of people living in reaction to pain.

Rebellion Is a Behavior, Not an Identity

Rebellion is a word that has such a negative connotation that most of us who love Jesus would never think it could creep into our way of thinking. One of the subtlest forms of rebellion is driven by selective hearing. People who are rebellious cannot be a light to the world because they're too busy trying to create their own light to shine to the world. Once, Eric from Epic Life corrected me for being disobedient. Initially I didn't know what he was talking about, but after spending some time with God about the issue, I remembered a conversation he and I had in which I only listened to what I wanted to hear.

This revelation shocked me because at that point, I wondered how many other times I had had selective hearing with people. The things I wanted to hear from my conversation with him, I remembered, but the things I didn't want to hear went in one ear and out the other. Rebellion plays a huge role when it comes to quenching the move of the Holy Spirit. Love is not rebellious; in fact, the love and the goodness of God casts out the rebellious spirit. *Do not remember the sins of my youth and my rebellious ways; according to your love remember me, for you, LORD, are good* (Psalms 25:7). After talking with Eric, I asked God why I had selective hearing in this particular situation and where this way of thinking originated. The Lord revealed something very powerful to me about my way of thinking. He told me that the reason I had selective hearing in this situation was because it reminded me of someone from my past that was verbally abusive and controlling toward me.

Because I didn't want to be controlled and manipulated by people anymore, the memory of what Eric told me not to do was suppressed, and I did what I wanted to do instead. I didn't have a problem with my leadership team; I had a problem with someone from my past who manipulated and abused me, and I was punishing the people on my leadership team for something someone else did to me a long time ago. The first thing I did was forgive the person who abused me long ago. Then I became thankful to Eric for his correction because had he not done this, I would never have been able to weed out that immature part of my character. God designed the human body with an amazing ability to protect itself from dangerous experiences. If I touch the fire on the stove and get burned, I will never want to touch a hot stove again. It's a great thing for our minds to transform to keep us safe from dangerous situations, but when it comes to people, we cannot think the same way.

Punishing the people we're in relationships with for something someone else did to us a long time ago is a very unhealthy way to live. Much of rebellion is rooted in a fear of being controlled, so to protect ourselves from being controlled and manipulated, some of us actually *become* controlling and manipulative. It's ironic, but by being rebellious, we end up becoming the very thing that we're trying to protect ourselves from. Many people think of their rebellion as a badge of honor instead of seeing it for its truly destructive nature.

On the contrary, as hard as it may be to accept, rebellion is very unhealthy, and it must be dealt with in truth, love, and the kindness of God; only then does transformation come. *Or do you show contempt for the riches of his kindness, forbearance and patience, not realizing that God's kindness is intended to lead you to repentance?* (Romans 2:4). To this day, I am very thankful to Eric for his correction, because it helped me in my personal life and continues to help me in my ministry as well. His correction, along with the correction of other powerful leaders in my life, has helped to guide me into the destiny God has planned for me.

Running from Fear

I used to think that running away from what scared me meant that I was running to God, but the truth is that running away from pain doesn't mean I'm running toward anything. I've often thought about the scene from *Jurassic Park* in which everyone is running away from all the dinosaurs. I would then think to myself, where exactly are they going? If I'm running away from a dinosaur, I want to make sure I'm running toward safety! Many of us go through life running away from the pain of our past, but we're not really running toward anything. We then wonder why we aren't making a difference in the world. We won't make it to the Promised Land by looking in the rearview mirror. A warrior that runs away from a battle isn't getting any closer to seeing victory. At a certain point, we must turn around and colabor with Christ as we fight off the old thought patterns the devil has been using to control us. One great way to break new ground and be the light that Jesus called us to be is by facing our demons.

A guy I know was born and raised in another country. He was involved in church ministry for several years and was repeatedly abused in his particular ministry. He used to be on their leadership team, but they started developing social clubs in their church and would exclude him from their leadership meetings. I can understand why he was hurt, but then he told me that "all churches are the same." Because of his bad experience at this one church, he hasn't been back to church since then. He also won't live in a community with other believers because he thinks that all people who go to church are hypocrites. He told me that he's tried going to different churches since his bad experience, but he feels that they're all the same. Because of his experiences, he developed a victim mentality, and he doesn't believe that he can be a light to the world the way Jesus has called us to. It really breaks my heart to know that there are many other people who think like this in the world. The first step to becoming a light to the world is to actually believe you can/will be a light to the world. If you don't believe you can be a light to the world, then ask the Holy Spirit why, and He will certainly help you to see beyond the lies and encounter the transforming love of the Father.

A few years ago, I was taking a Christ Life class at Epic Life. I read something in the phase-two book that changed my life forever. There was a story about a man who was having lots of problems, so he moved to another location. As soon as the man set foot in the new land, he was excited and looking forward to starting a whole new life. However, after only a short period of time of living in this new land, the man was having the same problems he'd had in the first place he was living. Thinking, again, that his location was the problem, he moved to another land even further away from the first two places he had lived. After only a short period of time, the man became very frustrated because, for the third time, the same problems occurred. Finally, the man realized that the problem wasn't his location. He realized that he was the one who had the problems, and he brought his mess with him everywhere he went.

I believe this is the way a lot of us do relationships. A lot of people will find something wrong with the person they're in a relationship with. They run away, thinking it's going to be different with another person, only to find the same problems with a new person. We can't be a light to the world if we can't even be a light to each other. When we learn how to build and sustain intimacy in our relationships with each other by dealing with fear, in love, then we will be able to shine our light in the darkness of the world.

Many times dark people can be scary, but if we shine our light using the power of His love, we will begin to make a difference in the lives of the "unreachable." Elizabeth Reisinger, a friend of mine who serves at Bethel Church in Redding, California, once said, "Escapism rarely leads to fruit. Rather than running from pain, run into it. Let God's big arms hold you in it. Healing happens in that moment when you allow yourself to slow down enough from busyness to feel and become aware of your heart's needs."

CHAPTER 5

The Power of the Tongue

*"Not everyone is able to solve problems in the heat of the
moment. I should not become angry with people who
don't process their emotions when I want them to."*

A Time to Be Silent

*There is a time for everything, and a season for every activity under
the heavens: a time to be silent and a time to speak* (Ecclesiastes
3:1 and 7b). There is power in the words we speak—power to
speak life, power to speak death, or power to say nothing at all. I
used to think that I always had to say something to be powerful.
I used to think that many words meant that people would understand who I am, how I think, or why I do the things I do. But I've
been learning over the years that sometimes, it's our many words
that get us into trouble. One of the best examples of what I'm talking about is in Matthew 27:12–14, which says, *When he was accused
by the chief priests and the elders, he gave no answer. Then Pilate asked
him, "Don't you hear the testimony they are bringing against you?" But Jesus
made no reply, not even to a single charge—to the great amazement of the
governor.* Jesus knew when it was His time to die on the cross, and I

believe had he spoken too soon, He would have been killed before fulfilling the destiny God had planned for Him.

At a new job, I had a manager named Jim who liked to "rough up" his new associates so that they would learn how to be strong in the workplace. While I understand why he treated me this way, and I'm sure he had good intentions, I was not OK with the verbal abuse. One day I asked him if I could work with one of the customers on my own without any assistance so that I could get more experience. Jim said, "Do you really think you're ready to do this on your own?"

I answered, "Yes, I am, but I want one of you to shadow me in case I say or do something wrong." The truth was that I wasn't ready, but I wanted to do it and ask questions along the way—that is the fastest way I learn. I told Jim that I learn fastest with hands-on experience, but he insisted on me watching one of the other associates work with customers for a few weeks. He wanted me to work with customers on my own after that. Even though I know it takes me a lot longer to learn something new that way, I did what my manager said.

After a few days of me watching my other associates work with the customers, Jim said, "Do you think you're ready to work with customers?"

Surprised by his question, I replied, "Yes, absolutely!"

Jim told me that a customer was coming in within the next few minutes and that I was going to take care of him. When the customer finally walked into the store, I walked over nervously and asked how I could help. Since I was new, I stumbled on many of my words, but eventually I ended up closing the sale. After the customer walked out of the store, I felt good about myself and was happy to have conquered that fear. About an hour after the customer left, Jim asked me how well I thought I had done. I told Jim that I felt confident that I did a good job. Then he said, "Are you sure that you think you did well?"

Perplexed that he was asking me the same question twice, I said, "Yes, I believe I did well."

Jim smiled cynically. "You didn't do well at all. You messed up a lot during that transaction."

I was really confused. I asked him what I had done wrong.

Jim took my final paperwork that I had printed for the customer. He went into the computer system and added a lot of other things to the customer's bill. He printed out his copy of the transaction and compared it to mine. The total price on my final bill was a lot less than the price on his bill. He asked me again, in a sarcastic tone, "Do you still think you're ready to work with customers?"

I wanted to tell him yes. Not because I wanted to be sarcastic, but because I wanted to learn from my mistake and try again. However, in a split second, I heard the Holy Spirit tell me not to say anything. I usually have a lot to say, but in this particular situation, I felt the Lord telling me that saying nothing was the perfect response. The reason I chose not to respond wasn't because I didn't think I had a voice. I chose not to respond because I didn't have anything to say that would have rectified the situation. As much as I didn't like that situation, Jim eventually grew to like me as an employee. I believe this happened because I was obedient in the times when the Lord told me to stay silent.

When I think about remaining silent, I think about love being patient. I don't believe that remaining silent means that we need to stay quiet and put up with an injustice. But what I do believe it means is that we need to wait to speak when God wants us to speak and remain silent when He wants us to remain silent. Sometimes the right answer is no answer because the timing is wrong. Love is patient, and it waits for the right time to speak up. Just like in the Scriptures, in which Jesus could have spoken up too soon and possibly gotten himself killed prior to him dying on the cross, I believe there is a right time for us to speak in our relationships with people. Not everyone is able to solve problems in the heat of the moment. I should not become angry with people who don't process their emotions when I want them to. Ephesians 4:26 says, *In your anger do not sin: do not let the sun go down while you are still angry.* I believe that this verse gives us a great example of how to manage relationships with people.

Based on that verse, I think that when we become angry, it is perfectly OK to walk away from a heated moment, but eventually we should come together again and discuss the matter. I think this verse gives us a good principle to live by: we shouldn't remain angry with someone, if at all possible, for more than a day. I believe this is a good *principle,* not a law. I believe the time to be silent in our relationships with people is when we need to be patient in God's love and wait for His timing to speak His heart through ours, into theirs. By no means does remaining silent mean that we keep quiet and hope the other person will figure out what's wrong with us.

This is a very immature way to think. We don't have super-natural powers to figure out what's going on in each other's heads without communicating our feelings with one another. We need to communicate—especially when we intentionally avoid communicating with one another for a period of time. When the decision to take a breather from a heated conversation is mutually made, both people in that relationship are able to process the situation in the quietness of their secret place with God. When that happens, they're empowered to come together again to discuss the matter being led by the Spirit instead of by their emotions.

Love Doesn't Hold Its Tongue

The tongue has the power of life and death, and those who love it will eat its fruit (Proverbs 18:21). Just like there is a time to be silent, there is also a time to speak up. A few years ago, as of this writing, I was at a restaurant with three friends. My friends Randy and Sarah had been in a rocky relationship with one another at that time, but I was happy to see them together. My third friend, Steve, had known us all for a long time. We sat down at a table and talked. Our food arrived, and we'd been eating and talking for a while. Steve asked Randy about a girl Randy had dated while he was broken up with Sarah. Sarah stopped smiling. She looked at Randy as if she had seen a ghost. Things got very quiet at the table for a few seconds. Steve said, "Come on, Sarah! You didn't know Randy was dating someone else while you guys were broken up?"

Steve continued to say a lot of other things to Randy that were very inappropriate, and Randy felt very ashamed and uncomfortable. I thought, "Is this really happening right now? Am I really in the middle of this?" The conversation between Randy and Steve progressively got more intense, and it seemed as if Sarah was feeling very uncomfortable. Finally, I had had enough of the nonsense. I interrupted everyone by saying loudly and firmly, "This conversation is completely inappropriate, and it needs to end right now!" Gossip is something I will not put up with.

Randy and his girlfriend Sarah moved to another table to talk to each other, and Steve just looked at me, dumbfounded. Steve, seemingly oblivious to what he did wrong, said to me, "I guess some people just can't handle the truth. I wish it hadn't gotten to this point."

"No Steve. That's not the problem. You were wrong for bringing up a past dating relationship Randy had with another woman. That's not something you bring up with his girlfriend, Sarah, sitting next to him. That's something you need to talk about with Randy one-on-one. What Randy did when he and Sarah were broken up is his business as long as he remains faithful to Sarah now that they're together. Does that make sense?" Steve nodded his head, and I could tell that he was starting to get it. The three of them didn't talk to each other at all the rest of the night, but later that week, Randy told me that Steve apologized to him, and they had reconciled. Love doesn't keep a record of wrongs, and I believe gossip is a very destructive and demonic spirit that wars against unadulterated love. As I mentioned in the beginning of the chapter, our words have the power to speak life or death into our relationships. Powerless people think that gossip is a way to guard the hearts of their loved ones, but the truth is that the only person who can guard your heart is you. No one else can do it for you. Whenever someone tells me that a manager is verbally abusing his associates, a neighbor is cheating on his wife, or a pastor said something wrong,

I say to that person, "I'm so sorry you're experiencing that. What are you going to do about it?"

Sometimes when I say this, people get confused because they think I'm going to continue to listen to gossip and be OK with that. The reason I ask people this question is because I want to empower them to believe they have the mind of Christ, and that through them, God will shift those circumstances. I've had people get offended when I ask them to talk to the person they have a problem with, because they expect me to solve their problems for them. When I become a problem solver in someone else's life, I also become his or her savior, which is supposed to be Jesus's job. Love doesn't hold its tongue in the face of injustice. Instead, it calls people out of an orphan-and-victim mentality and into a son-daughter identity. True love will set boundaries in relationships. People may run from our boundaries, but true love will also take them back unconditionally; it's the epitome of the message in "The Prodigal Son" (see Luke 15:11–32).

Some years ago, while I was in ministry, I became afraid of sharing what God put in my heart. I was afraid because I didn't want people to think that I thought I was better than them. When I pray for someone, God usually gives me a picture or a scenario in my head about something that's going on in the other person's life. While in ministry, I've had some people tell me that my prophetic words are driven by a spirit of performance. They said that I was trying to draw attention to myself. Certain people, both in and out of the church, didn't like me very much. When I noticed that I was drawing negative attention to myself when I stepped out in faith, I watered down my prayers. For a season, I stopped praying for healing, and I stopped giving people prophetic words because I didn't want people to think I was arrogant. I rarely prayed for people, and whenever I did, it was a generic prayer. I would still get prophetic words and words of knowledge for people in my head, but I chose not to share what the Lord was *really* saying.

For the longest time, I used to think that having a spirit of performance only applied to people who seek attention in unhealthy ways. But I learned that it also applies to those who are afraid to disappoint people. The truth is that I did have a spirit of performance because I cared too much about what the wrong people thought about me. In ministry back then and even today, I hold myself accountable to the leaders of my church. Because my leaders always supported me in ministry, I knew that I wasn't praying for people with wrong motives. One thing I have changed about the way I do ministry today is to stop caring about what the wrong people think. Bill Johnson has said, "If you don't live by the praise of men, you won't die by their criticism." This bad experience silenced me for the wrong reasons. Love has to be brave. It has to keep believing even when it hurts, and it has to speak up because it understands the supernatural power of life in the tongue.

The Power of Words

And God said, "Let there be light," and there was light (Genesis 1:3). Words aren't just powerful enough to speak life into existence, but they also breathe life into our relationships with people. I remember a night I met with two of my brothers in Christ for fellowship at a coffee shop. Eli and Alex are two very powerful men of God who come from very different walks of life, but they both have amazing testimonies. That night, I shared some struggles with my brothers about how God had healed me from some terrible experiences I had with a friend from my past. I shared with Eli and Alex that I had had a strange dream about my friend that seemed very dark; I wanted some clarification as to its meaning. Eli, being very prophetic, interpreted the dream in a way that was completely different from what I felt the dream meant. I was taken aback by the revelation because not only did it align with the heart of God, but it also gave me a better perspective about the dream.

After Eli shared his interpretation of my dream, Alex shared his powerful testimony about how God was using a bad experience he had had with someone from his past to make a difference in people's lives. This was such a powerful night for me because I felt like our spirits bonded to each other (read 1 Samuel, chapter 18). During our time of fellowship, there was a sense of peace in my heart that I couldn't explain. Before we left the coffee shop, we all prayed and prophesied over each other. After the prayer, I felt like I was having an out-of-body experience. I felt so alive that the feeling was almost overwhelming. *Again, truly I tell you that if two of you on earth agree about anything they ask for, it will be done for them by my Father in heaven* (Matthew 18:19). The words we speak can declare life and healing over a tough situation. I believe the power of community is how we gain the strength we need from the Lord to fight the lies of the enemy that come during an isolated moment of weakness.

Sometimes I lie in my bed at night and listen to recordings of prophetic words that people have given me throughout the years. For me, this is such a powerful thing because it reminds me every day of what God wants to do in my life. There have been days that I just felt like wallowing in my sorrow because of a situation that didn't appear to be getting any better, but I would force myself to listen to recordings of prophetic words throughout the day. Doing this aligned my feelings with the truth of who Jesus is and what He has called me to do in my life.

One of the ways that words can speak life into existence is through our thoughts. *We demolish arguments and every pretension that sets itself up against the knowledge of God, and we take captive every thought to make it obedient to Christ* (2 Corinthians 10:5). There was a time that a female friend and I were prophesying over someone. After we both finished praying, the person we prayed for confirmed that everything my friend said was completely accurate. I felt jealous because my friend's prophetic word was more accurate than mine. She is a very humble person, so I knew that feeling jealous was my own problem. On my way home, I started talking to God about the situation. I *knew* I was wrong for feeling jealous toward her, so I asked God what I needed to do about it. The Lord told me, *I want you to prophesy over her right-now.*

When I heard God say that, it felt like someone had punched me in the stomach. The last thing in the world I wanted to do was to prophesy over someone I was jealous of, but I wanted to be obedient, so I prophesied over her. The words the Lord gave me for her were as follows: *You will be a healing/prophesying evangelist. You will travel the nations and do greater works than both Jesus and Ernesto combined.* When I heard the Lord tell me that He wanted to bless her in that way, my pride was destroyed. The powerful thing about this experience is that the more I continued to prophesy over my amazing friend, the more my feelings agreed with what God was saying. Finally, after a few minutes of praying for her, I actually did want all of those things to happen for her. I was filled with joy! Just because a thought of jealousy popped into my head didn't mean that I was going to agree with that thought. I believe that taking thoughts captive means that we choose to reject the way a thought makes us feel by speaking out His truth.

Another way that words can speak life is by praying in the Spirit (read Ephesians 6:18). One day I was driving home from work, really exhausted and not in the best mood, and the Lord told me to go to the grocery store and give someone a word of knowledge. I really wasn't in the mood to do that, and honestly, I just wanted to go home. I felt as if the Lord wanted me to start praying, aloud, in the Spirit. I didn't feel like doing that either, but I did as the Lord asked. After praying for a while, I felt a peace come over me that I couldn't explain. When I got to the grocery store, I couldn't wait to ask God who He wanted me to share His love with. The first thing the Holy Spirit showed me in my mind was a picture of green bell peppers, so I knew that's where I needed to go (I didn't even need to buy bell peppers). After I finished buying everything I needed, I went to the green bell peppers and spotted an older woman. While I shared the word of knowledge with her, she seemed shocked and surprised that this was even happening. But she was thankful for the blessing, and I was blessed as well.

When we do what we want, we only go to the grocery store to buy groceries. But when we do what the Lord wants, we go to the grocery store to show someone His love through the power of His words spoken through us. When we speak life into our relationships with people, love flows from those relationships into the lives of others. Many of us choose to live based on whether or not something feels right or wrong. But the truth, as I quoted from Banning Liebscher in chapter 1, is that truth isn't anchored in our feelings; truth is anchored in Scripture. When we entertain negative thoughts, the words we speak will mimic those thoughts. But when we train our minds to be transformed by His truth, our negative thoughts will be held captive by His grace. His love and grace are what change the way we think. I believe that without love, it is impossible to speak life, because love has to look like more than positive thinking—it has to look like Jesus.

Words become realities when love is the motivating force. It's easier to say what we're feeling, especially if it's something negative, but it's impossible to take back what's already been said. Many of us say things we don't really mean because we're letting our emotions control our lives. When our emotions control the way we think, not even God can help us. When my voice is louder than His, Jesus cannot bring the change I desire into my relationships. Love is teachable. God doesn't only speak to us through direct revelation, but He also speaks to us through imperfect people. When we are not open to receiving feedback from the people God puts in our lives, we render ourselves powerless in our relationships. I believe that when we use the power of the tongue to speak life into our relationships with people, we will no longer create walls between each other to protect ourselves from the other person. Instead, we will rearrange our boundaries so that both of us are able to receive love in a safe and healthy way.

CHAPTER 6

Love and Boundaries

"Telling codependent people that they have authority through Christ to set their own boundaries is usually offensive to them. The reason they become offended is because they believe it is someone else's job to maintain their happiness."

Filtering Noise in Relationships

It's easy to put a priority on something important that isolates us from the people who matter the most. Scripture tells us to *love your neighbor as yourself* (Mark 12:31). I believe one of the ways we need to love ourselves is by setting boundaries that make time for covenant relationships. If we do not learn how to take control of our lives, other people will be more than happy to take control of it for us. There is a lot of need in our world. Everybody is always going to need something, but it's up to us to choose when we'll sacrifice and when we'll be filled up (read John 12:8).

When Jesus walked the earth, He was never overwhelmed by the crowd because He was constantly living in response to what the Father was saying. Living in reaction to everything people are telling us creates noise in our relationships with people. This noise makes it difficult for us to stay connected with the people who matter the most. One way we can filter the noise in our relationships is by learning how to say no to people and things. One of the greatest detriments to setting healthy boundaries is the people-pleasing mentality. The people-pleasing mentality thrives in codependent relationships. A person who is codependent will require a people pleaser to meet all of his or her emotional and spiritual needs whenever needed. People who are codependent will not only suck the life out of people who are people pleasers, but they will also run over their boundaries and consume their lives with problems that never seem to have solutions.

I used to be a people pleaser. What I've experienced personally with people who are codependent is that so much of my time was spent delving into their lives until I didn't have any time to connect with people who actually delved into *my* life. To take control of my life, I empowered these people to set boundaries in their own lives through the power of the Holy Spirit. Telling codependent people that they have authority through Christ to set their own boundaries is usually offensive to them. The reason they become offended is because they believe it is someone else's job to maintain their happiness. I think that people who are codependent can become controlling when they don't get their way in a relationship. Codependency is a thought process that branches from the victim mentality, and people who think like victims will use control and manipulation to make powerful people feel like their boundaries are selfish. As sons and daughters of God, we must resist the temptation to become offended when we recognize control and manipulation in these people.

When we know who we are in Christ, we will not react to disrespectful conversations, but we will choose to respond in love, regardless of the situation. I love to help people, and I love to see people step into their destiny. But when I prioritize helping people over my covenant relationships, burnout is the repercussion. I've gotten very close to that point before. Then I learned, through many powerful leaders in my life, how to set boundaries on how many people I will help and when I'll help them. I believe one of the best ways to filter the noise in our covenant relationships is by setting boundaries that put a priority on our personal covenant friendships.

Making Sacrifices

Just like learning how to say no to people is essential to maintaining a healthy balance in our relationships, learning when to say yes is just as important, especially when it's inconvenient. I am very busy throughout a typical week, but I am very intentional about everything I do. While writing this book, I felt the Lord telling me to spend one day of my week writing and spending time in His presence. One day, a friend asked me if I would be available to help her move into a new apartment. I didn't know how to respond to her because it was the same day God had asked me to spend time with Him. I asked the Holy Spirit what to do, and He told me, *I want you to help your friend move.*

I responded to the Lord. "But God, didn't you say that day was for me to spend time with you?"

The Lord said, *Yes, but you need to help your friend on that day, and I want you to cancel the two events you're planning tonight so you can spend time with Me.*

I was shocked, but I said, "Yes, Lord!" I didn't really want to cancel the two events because I had already committed to them, but I've learned throughout the years to always be obedient to God, even when I don't understand.

After cancelling the two events, I spent time writing and resting in God's presence. The next day I helped my friend move into her new apartment and then spent the rest of the day writing and soaking in the presence of the Lord. It may be true that man plans his ways, but if our plan is so rigid that there's no room for God to determine our steps, it probably means we're trying to strive and determine our own steps (Proverbs 16:9). I made a plan about how my schedule was going to look according to what God had told me, but then God changed my plan by reminding me that He lives in a realm outside of time. A "day" can mean whatever He wants it to mean (2 Peter 3:8). In this specific situation, God told me to dedicate one day during the week to spend time with Him. But later He told me to cancel some events I had planned and to help my friend move on the same day He told me to spend time with Him. Putting other people before ourselves is a great example of "dying to ourselves" as Scripture states. We don't die to ourselves by helping people because we think we're worthless; we do it because we know the difference He wants us to make in other people's lives will be worth it. Making sacrifices from a place of rest equips us for inconvenient situations in which God wants us to practice sacrificial love. When we sacrifice from a place of rest, the things God asks us to do will never be overwhelming. *The Lord replied, "My Presence will go with you, and I will give you rest"* (Exodus 33.14).

When I was younger, I used to believe sacrificing meant that other people were more important than me. I felt like I had to go to certain activities or events because I didn't want to disappoint people. Today, whenever I feel as if God wants me to make a sacrifice, I don't do it to avoid hurting people's feelings. I do it because I want to be obedient to what God is saying. The difference is that when I try not to disappoint people, my self-worth is based on what other people think of me instead of it being on what Jesus thinks of me. On the other hand, when I'm simply being obedient to what the Lord is saying, my sacrifice isn't because I don't want to disappoint people—it's because I love God, and I want to see people healed and set free like He does.

Boundaries Create Connection

Above all else, guard your heart, for everything you do flows from it (Proverbs 4:23). The reason we guard our hearts isn't because we want to push people away; it's because we want to keep fear out and let love and intimacy flow in. I have learned this the hard way time and time again. I believe guarding our hearts means to pursue intimacy with people to the degree that they are able to receive love. This is hard to do because there have been many times that I wanted my relationship with a particular person to look a certain way, but the other person wasn't receptive. There have been brothers in Christ that I wanted to get to know better. I would contact them and ask them to meet up, but for whatever reason, they were unable to connect with me in a way I would have liked. In situations like these, I choose to respect their boundaries and continue to pursue a connection with them in the way that guards both of our hearts. Honoring everyone's boundaries allows a foundation of love and respect to be established.

When people who we used to be in covenant with start seeming more distant, it's easy for us to jump to conclusions without ever communicating with them. Many times, jumping to conclusions is the biggest reason why relationships fall apart. This type of thinking can also develop a self-righteous mentality: "Well, if this person is going to ignore me, then I don't want to be in relationship with him anyway. I deserve better than that!" We may not like or agree with someone who decides to become distant for whatever reason, but jumping to conclusions is never the answer. Disconnecting with people we don't agree with is not a boundary—it's pride. My focus should never be, "I deserve better than this." It should be, "I love you too much to allow miscommunication to hurt our relationship." Communication, paired with transparency and vulnerability, breeds intimacy. Just because my relationship with someone doesn't look the way I want it to look doesn't mean it can't be everything God wants it to be. A relationship is not about what I can get out of it; it's about what I can pour into it.

We cannot expect one person to meet all of our needs and then get offended when they don't meet our expectations. Jesus is the only person who will never disappoint us. We must also believe, without ceasing, the things He has promised us in Scripture. God promises that if we love and obey Him, He'll give us what we want (Psalms 37:4). He tells us that if we remain humble, we will inherit the earth (Matthew 5:5). And He tells us that when we spend time in His presence in the secret place, we will be rewarded in the public place (Matthew 6:6 KJV). When God promises us these things, one of the main ways to see them come to fruition is to never give up until what He said becomes our reality. We should never create expectations for people, because we end up putting them on the pedestal that God is supposed to be on. I believe there is a direct connection between guarding our hearts, expectancy, and desires coming into realization.

Guarding our hearts doesn't protect us from a disappointment, since trust involves risk. However, it does protect us from unhealthy relationships with no boundaries. Setting boundaries on our hearts creates a culture of expectancy in our relationships with people. Kris Vallotton has broken down the difference between expectations and expectancy, and the difference is huge. My take on what Kris said is that having expectations defers hope, because the focus is on the fact that I want this relationship to look a certain way. Yet expectancy restores hope, because it focuses on the fact that God will give us exactly what we want even if it doesn't look the way we want. Expectancy restores the hope that expectations defer. When we guard our hearts with a sense of expectancy, we won't be protected from experiencing disappointments. But with the right attitude and through perseverance, we will be positioned to receive and steward the deepest desires of our hearts. Boundaries keep us connected with the people we love even if our relationship with them doesn't look the way we want. Love doesn't demand its own way, but if it's real, it will never fail when it's put to the test.

While I do believe there are times that we must stay away from people who constantly disrespect our boundaries and refuse to repent, our purpose for setting boundaries should always be to build healthy connections with people. In the past, I have been hurt by friends who gossiped about me. I've been scarred by unhealthy dating relationships, and I've been verbally abused by managers who misused their authority. Because of all my bad experiences with people, I got to the point one day when I said, "I think it would be better if I could go back in time to when I never knew any of the people who hurt me. I would be much better off today if I never had all of these painful memories playing in my head over and over again like a video without a *stop* button. I wish I had never known any of those people."

The same night I said that, the Lord gave me a dream. In the dream, I walked into a room and saw a good friend of mine sitting down, relaxing. I knew that I had gone back in time so that we could fix the mistakes we made with each other. I said, "Hey! What's up? How are you?"

"Hello there! My name is Andy." I was confused that my friend was introducing himself to me as if I didn't know him, but the truth was…I didn't. In this dream, I had gone back in time so far that I had never even met him yet.

"I'm Ernesto! You don't remember me?"

"This is my first time meeting you. I've got to go because I've got some things I need to take care of; see you later."

When I woke up, I heard the Lord tell me that the reason He doesn't allow us to change the past is because the pain of not being known can be worse than the pain caused by the mistakes we've made. It's better for relationships to be real and messy than it is for them to be nonexistent. Making an attempt to reconcile is better than never being known at all. It's easy to think that cleaning up our mistakes would be more painful than abandoning a painful relationship, but the Lord revealed to me through this dream that losing a connection with someone would actually be a more painful experience. It is better for us to reconcile with the people who've hurt us than it is to go back in time and not be known at all. While we can't change the past, and I don't believe we would want to, we can change the future by choosing to use the power of boundaries and vulnerability to stay connected with the people we love. *If it is possible, as far as it depends on you, live at peace with everyone* (Romans 12:18). Choosing to create boundaries that will strengthen our relationships with people is a high call, but it always reaps a great reward.

Love Always Trusts

Love always trusts God, regardless of past disappointments. One early morning, I was looking out my window. I was looking at a bird on top of my neighbor's roof. As we all know, birds will fly away at the slightest noise or movement. As I watched this bird through the window, I thought, "If I try to get that bird to land on my shoulder, it wouldn't happen, because that bird doesn't trust me." Generally, birds will not choose to land on moving targets. This is because landing on a moving target is unpredictable unless a foundation of trust has been previously established. When it comes to trusting God, many of us are waiting for God to create a stationary landing pad before we decide to trust Him in what He's called us to step into. In the early stages of the Christian life, I do believe God works this way, but as we begin to go deeper into developing our relationship with Him, He calls us into a level of trust that requires us to land on "moving targets."

Because God will ask us to land on moving targets, we might feel that we aren't ready to fully step into what God is calling us into. If we wait until we're ready, most of us will never do what God has called us to. But if we wait until we're fully willing, we step into a lifestyle of breakthrough because of our radical obedience. If God said it, not only is He going to provide for it, but He's also going to sustain it. I believe that many of us don't fully step into our divine assignment, because we are setting boundaries with God based on past disappointments with people. It's absolutely necessary for us to set boundaries with people, but we should not be setting boundaries with God. When it comes to people, trust is something that has to be earned. However, trust is the nature of who God is, so it doesn't need to be earned. Many times, trusting God can be scary as hell, but our obedience will open up the heavens.

One day I went to an auto-repair shop that I used to work for to get an oil change. While I was there, I struck up a conversation with some of the employees—my previous colleagues. They asked me questions about my previous book, *Why Christians Are Skeptical of the Supernatural*, so I shared with them how blessed I felt to be able to make a difference in the people's lives that were reading it. I noticed an older woman watching us and listening to what we were saying. After the service advisor wrote the work order for my oil change, I took a seat in the waiting room. The same woman walked into the waiting room and sat down. After a few minutes, she started talking to me about a book she was reading. As our conversation progressed, she eventually told me about how many times she had been disappointed in her relationships.

She said to me, "Ernesto, I have been divorced twice, and I was abused in both of those marriages. My first husband was a Christian man who went to church, read the Bible and all of that, but He didn't treat me right. After having that terrible experience with him, we eventually divorced, and sometime later I decided to marry a nonbeliever. My second marriage started off great, just like my first, but eventually my second husband abused me too, so we divorced. I am a Christian, I believe in Jesus just like you do, and I believe God has been telling me that the reason marriage hasn't worked out for me is because men cannot be trusted. Please don't be offended—I'm sure you're a great guy—but God has been showing me through the years that I am not supposed to be married because men can't be fully trusted." As the woman shared this with me, I looked at her and listened to the sound of her broken heart through her words. I didn't nod, I didn't agree—I just listened. When my oil change was finished, I paid the bill, and then the Lord told me that He wanted me to give her a word of knowledge. I blessed the woman with a word of knowledge, then made my way to my car.

As I was driving home, my heart broke for her. To this day, I can't even imagine the pain she was going through, having been through two abusive marriages. While I do believe that a few people are called to live a life of celibacy, I don't believe this type of revelation comes from bad experiences. I have talked to many people who suffer from posttraumatic stress disorder (PTSD) because of pain caused by extremely unhealthy relationships. Scientific research has proven that PTSD changes the physical makeup of the human brain. PTSD changes God's truth until it begins to sound like one's own truth. I personally believe that PTSD is one of the main reasons why people set boundaries with God. Without the power of the Holy Spirit, people who suffer from PTSD are physically unable to change the way they think. I believe that radical obedience to God supernaturally destroys the power of PTSD. The renewing of the mind is a spiritual truth that transforms the minds of people who have been altered by PTSD. It's such a powerful principle that it physically corrects and restores the makeup of the human brain back to the way God intended it to be.

A few years prior to writing this book, I dated a woman named Veronica, who I mentioned in chapter 3. The first time we went on a date, we went to a specific coffee shop. As time went on, that relationship failed, and it was a very painful time for me. I caught myself avoiding the same places where she and I had gone on dates. There were so many painful memories that flooded my mind when I went to those places that it was almost unbearable. The Holy Spirit told me to start meeting with friends at the same coffee shop Veronica and I had gone to. I immediately told God, "OK, I'm setting a boundary! I will no longer go to the places Veronica and I went to anymore because it hurts too much to be in that environment!"

The Lord said to me gently, *Son, that's why I want you to go back to all of those places—because I don't want those experiences to control your life.* I can remember feeling extremely oppressed because I could not believe He would make me do something like that. Even though I didn't want to go back to the places Veronica and I had gone, I did, and I created new memories with new friends.

I didn't "feel" like being obedient, but it was my obedience to God that led me to forgive Veronica for her mistakes, to forgive myself for my mistakes, and to continue to see her to this day as my sister in Christ. Disobedience will never take you to the Promised Land. No matter how much it hurts to be obedient, choose vulnerability, choose transparency, and choose love. Obedience is like a shot of penicillin to a wound; it hurts when applied, but it eventually eliminates deeply rooted wounds and brings complete restoration for those who persevere. Today, whenever I go back to the same places Veronica and I had gone, the memories of what happened sometimes still pop up in my head, but there is no painful association with those memories anymore. Whenever we think we are setting boundaries with God, the truth is that we are actually creating walls that will prevent God from giving us the desires of our heart. Relationships become healthy when we remove boundaries with God, set healthy boundaries with people, and run into Daddy God's arms in the face of pain rather than running away. Sometimes it's the areas of our lives where fear is in control that God hides the keys that will unlock the deepest desires of our heart (read Jeremiah 29:13). Boundaries keep us away from the road that leads to a life full of pain and disappointment. In turn, we are drawn closer to a tree of life that abounds in love and desires brought fully into realization.

CHAPTER 7

The Father's Heart

*"God the Father can always be trusted, but we can only
receive life in abundance to the measure that we believe
He can be trusted."*

The Importance of Sonship

We cannot truly be fathers without knowing how to be sons
or daughters first. Being a son is about receiving, and being
a father is about equipping our children with what we've received. I
believe that becoming a father is much more than just having biological
children. It's about preparing children for their divine destiny. Many
of us think that being a father starts when we have children of our
own, but I believe that being a father can start when we adopt spiritual
children. God did not create us to be orphans and victims; He created
us to be sons and daughters that will become fathers and mothers who
will raise more sons and daughters. When I was younger, my idea of
fathering people was to tell them what they were doing wrong so that
they could do what I wanted them to do. There are many broken people in this world, and God wants to use those of us who know who we
are in Christ to speak into their lives as spiritual mothers and fathers.

To backtrack a little, the idea of being a spiritual father or even having a spiritual father is fairly new to me. I've only embraced it in the past year of my life as of this writing. I was born into a great family, with parents who love me very much, but having spiritual mothers and fathers is a completely different concept. It's one thing to be born into a family, but it's another thing to choose a family. I lived my life as an orphan for twenty-three years. As of this writing, it's only in the past five years that I've started living my life as a child of God. Learning how to be a child of God is essential if we want to learn how to father people. A father who doesn't know how to receive like a child from his Daddy God will father people with what he has, which unfortunately is a whole lot of nothing. When it comes to being in relationship with people, many of us do the best we can with what we've learned from our parents. I believe, in this generation more than ever, that the Lord wants us to build a culture where we will no longer "do relationships the best way we know how." Instead, we will choose to take personal responsibility for our actions and choose to do relationships the way Jesus knows how.

The Orphan Mentality

People who live like orphans will make difficult decisions on their own because they don't believe they have a mother or father. Some mothers and fathers think that simply being around for their children or providing for them financially is good enough, but children need more than financial resources and physical presence from their parents—they need affection. This is one reason many children grow up thinking that they don't need God. Many children grow up with a father who doesn't know how to be affectionate toward them, and they think that God is the same way. One of the greatest dangers of the orphan mentality is that it prevents us from receiving the Father's promises. Just as there were giants in the Promised Land, there are also giants we will need to overcome when the Lord gives us the desires of our heart. Orphans who don't know how to receive the love of God the Father will never feel like they belong anywhere.

After I attempted suicide, as described in chapter 3, it took a long time for me to be OK with staying in the same geographical location. My initial thought after that traumatic experience was that I needed to move far away. I knew that I was a child of God, but fear has a way of making an orphan mentality rise to the surface. Even though I had lots of friends and family who supported me through that emotionally challenging time, I still had a hard time receiving their love. Around October of 2014, I felt the Lord putting it on my heart to build community with Jesus Culture Sacramento. This was a scary thought for me because I had been part of Epic Life for four years, and I couldn't imagine having to start building community with people all over again.

Though Jesus Culture has the same DNA as Epic Life, my first few months at JC Sacramento were rough because I was completely out of my comfort zone. As time went on, I asked the Lord how my transition could be a little easier. He sent me a vision of a house. In the vision, the house appeared to have many new rooms that were under construction. He told me that I wasn't *building* community; I was *extending* my community. I wasn't joining a new family—I was introducing my existing family to relatives they haven't met yet. While I am now a part of JC Sacramento, and I love my new family, I am still a part of my Epic Life family. I feel that one of the things that made connecting with people easier for me at JC Sacramento is that I decided to bring my existing family with me on this amazing journey the Lord has me on. Learning how to receive the Father's love as a son or daughter of God is so essential when it comes to living with a purpose. Many of us are trying to make a difference in the world as an orphan instead of as a son or daughter living in a community, but one of the best ways to make a difference in the world is by doing it with our chosen family.

Fathering People (Building a Legacy)

The challenges you overcome in the desert prepare you for the challenges you'll face in the Promised Land. Sons and daughters don't allow their bad experiences to define them; they let their bad experiences refine them. Orphans aren't capable of building legacies because they define themselves by what happens to them. But sons and daughters define themselves by the alignment of their thoughts with the authority given to them by the One who created them. I believe that building a legacy has to do with fathering the next generation. As of this writing, at twenty-eight, while I'm not a biological father yet, I have fathered many people younger than myself. Although I'm still in my twenties, my goal is to call people younger than myself into their God-given destiny. I want my ceiling to be the floor of those younger than me. I want junior-high and high-school students to know what I know now, so that when they get to be my age, they will be much wiser and better equipped to make a difference in the world that will impact the next generation. When we learn how to receive from the Father, that's when we learn how to spread the Father's love to those who need it the most. People who feel loved and valued will have the confidence to create the legacy God wants them to create.

When I was in high school, my father taught me how to work on cars and how to solve mathematical equations when I had trouble with my homework. When I turned eighteen, I wanted to go to automotive technical school to learn more about cars. My father never went to college, so his goal was for me to have better career opportunities than he had had. When I told my father that I wanted to go to technical school, he bought me a car and paid for my tuition. My father told me that he wanted me to have all of the things that he never had. I believe this is what building a legacy is all about. I believe that fathering people is more about being able to receive love from God the Father than it is about age. There are people in their fifties and sixties who still operate as orphans and choose to live in survival mode from day to day.

On the other hand, there are teenagers who have already had more bad experiences in their short lives than I have had. Yet they have chosen to be transformed by the renewing of their minds, and in turn, they're making an impact in this generation. Over the past year, God has been connecting me with many spiritual mentors/mothers and fathers much older than myself who have chosen to live and receive like sons and daughters. Love has to look like something, and I believe one of the things it looks like is fathering the next generation.

His Love Is Trustworthy

Many of us don't have a problem with the idea of trusting God, but we have a problem with trusting people. The problem with that mentality is that oftentimes, God speaks through imperfect people. It is impossible to trust God without trusting the imperfect people He speaks through. Over the past five years, I've tried to be consistent in meeting with people for coffee on a weekly basis. Many of these people are meeting with me for the first time. This first meeting always makes me a little nervous because I don't know if the person will actually show up. The reason that thought goes through my mind is because it's happened to me a few times in the past five years since I started doing this. Regardless of the negative experiences I've have had in the past with certain people, I believe love looks like always trusting God for the best in new relationships.

A few years ago, my friend Joe wanted to meet with me for coffee. At that time, I was living in Elk Grove, California, and we both agreed that we would meet in Sacramento. Because of traffic, it took me about forty-five minutes to get to the coffee shop. Joe wasn't there. Because this was my first time meeting with him, I was nervous. After waiting for about five minutes, I called Joe to find out what was going on, but Joe didn't answer. Finally, after about fifteen minutes, Joe called and said, "Ernesto! I'm so sorry, brother, but I don't think I'm going to be able to meet with you, because there's a lot of traffic."

"I know there's a lot of traffic, but I still showed up. I'm willing to wait for you; that's no problem at all."

Joe said, "Oh, I'm sorry that you already drove all the way out there. I feel really bad, but I won't be able to make it."

"Joe, you said you wanted to meet with me for coffee. I drove forty-five minutes to get here, and now you don't want to meet because there's too much traffic?"

"I know, man, and I feel really bad. I'm sorry, but I can't make it!"

Needless to say, I was very irritated with Joe. Even though I have never met with Joe for coffee since, I forgave him for what happened. A few years after that happened, Joe contacted me because he was planning an overseas mission trip to the Middle East, and he wanted me to help him with a donation. After talking to the Holy Spirit about it, I felt the Lord telling me to donate money toward his fundraiser even though I didn't have much money in my bank account because I wasn't working at that time.

Even though I knew I was supposed to donate money to my friend Joe, I wasn't sure how much to donate due to my tough financial situation. Shortly after Joe contacted me, a stranger from my church told me that he felt as if the Lord wanted him to give me $300. From the $300 I received from the stranger, I donated a portion toward Joe's overseas mission trip and saved the rest of it to sustain me financially. Joe went on his mission trip to the Middle East, and God used him in powerful ways to make a difference in the lives of the people he came in contact with. If I had stayed offended with Joe because he couldn't meet with me for coffee, I would not have had the opportunity to invest into a powerful move of the Holy Spirit in the Middle East years later. Sometimes, I believe God will test our character by asking us to invest into the lives of people who have hurt us in the past; trust looks like obedience, regardless of whether or not it feels like obedience.

A few weeks after I attempted suicide, as I shared in the beginning of chapter 3, I made a commitment to the Lord that I was going to fast for seven days for breakthroughs in every area of my life. Never in my entire life had I taken fasting so seriously. I was so tired of doing the same thing over and over again and expecting different results that I was ready to "die to myself" and live fully for Christ, giving myself no other options. I was tired of saying that I was a Christian while continuing to struggle with the same sins over and over again. At that time, I remembered the verse in which Jesus said that if our eye causes us to stumble that we should pluck it out to remain pure (Matthew 18:9). While I didn't think plucking my eyes out should be my first option, I knew I needed to do something drastic to let God know that I was serious about changing and trusting Him fully with all areas of my life.

For the first day of my fast, I did a Daniel fast (I only ate fruits and vegetables and drank lots of water) for about twenty hours. During that day I did a lot of reading. Unfortunately, toward the end of the twenty hours, I felt very dizzy and weak, and my body could no longer handle the food fast. Because of this, I knew I needed to change the way I fasted for the remaining days. For the next six days, I abstained from all social media and Internet. I didn't check any e-mails, and I abstained from all events and social gatherings. I only connected with people via phone, text, and one-on-one covenant relationships. I even paid all of my bills prior to the fast to avoid any distractions. The only things I did all day, every day, that week were reading, praying, worshiping, resting with God, and listening to sermons. I was ready to trust God in a way that I had never trusted Him before in my entire life.

While fasting should never be done for the purpose of appearing holy (Matthew 6:16), I believe that giving an example of what fasting looks like helps us to learn more about what "dying to ourselves" means; it looks different for everyone (read about Moses's fast in Deuteronomy, chapter 9). For me, dying to myself meant that I was ready to give up all worldly pleasures for the sake of trusting the Father with all of my heart. There are many people who never receive life in abundance as Jesus promised because they refuse to fully submit to Him. But for me, doing things my own way almost took my life, so the only option I gave myself was to trust Him. While I'm not perfect, and I still stumble from time to time, I refuse to go back to the person I was yesterday. The reason God wants us to sacrifice our hopes and dreams to follow Jesus is because He wants to give us hope and fulfill our dreams; it's ironic. I believe that it's easier to sacrifice everything for Him when we fully trust in everything He says.

In November of 2012, I had a dream in which I saw Jesus walking me into a kitchen where there was a demonic presence. For some reason, I knew I had been there before. In the dream, I remembered being in this same kitchen previously, and there were bugs crawling on the floor and demonic spirits that manifested in the natural realm. When Jesus led me into the kitchen, although there was darkness, there was no more demonic presence. Jesus led me to a fish tank that illuminated bright white. The light was so bright that it was blinding in a magnificent way. The fish tank was filled with many fish that I understood to be "people" the Lord had trusted with powerful gifts, but they never practiced their authority. There were only two fish that were praying, and Jesus pulled them out of the tank. Suddenly, Jesus and I were supernaturally transported to an open field with a large pond. As I stood next to Jesus, he put the two fish into the new pond, which had more opportunity. At first, they were confused, having never been in a pond that massive before. They didn't know what to do. However, after a while, one fish took the initiative to explore this new territory, and the other fish followed.

On a personal level, this dream means something very specific to me. Yet on a corporate level, I believe what God is doing in this generation is raising revivalists who are unafraid of putting the spiritual authority they've been given into practice. Using our spiritual authority to step into the unknown can look like preaching the Gospel in a nation that is resistant to the Gospel. It can look like a single mom who teaches her children how to carry the presence, love, and power of God with them for the first time to a school that believes God is dead. And it can even look like a couple that is on the verge of divorce stopping and saying to one another, "Let's try this marriage one more time." Fear of the unknown will never take you to your destiny, but obedience in the face of the unknown will always take you to your promise. God the Father can always be trusted, but we can only receive life in abundance to the measure that we believe He can be trusted.

Jesus Christ was a physical manifestation of the Father's love when He walked the earth, but God the Father *is* love. I believe that many times we want a relationship with Jesus, but we don't want a relationship with the Father because God the Father reminds us of our fathers. Many people don't want to be reminded of their father because memories of their father aren't the greatest. The truth is that regardless of whether your father was amazing or not so amazing, you are amazing. The relationship that Jesus had with God the Father is a perfect example of what our relationship should look like with God. Mark 14:36 quotes Jesus: *"Abba, Father," he said, "everything is possible for you. Take this cup from me. Yet not what I will, but what you will."* God isn't just the man in the sky who is far away from us in every way shape and form, but He is a Daddy who loves us and is a Father to the fatherless (Psalms 68:5).

It is so essential that we know how to receive from Daddy God the way Jesus did if we want to live the legacy that we were created for. I believe that it is intimacy with the Father in the secret place that releases the revival we cry out for in the public place. When we learn how to receive from God the Father as the little children of God that we are, we will be able to release the Father's love in practical ways that will change our schools, our cities, our governments, our nations, and our world. When our hearts become intertwined with His heart, we carry an anointing to heal the broken hearts of those who have a distorted view of what a father's love should look like.

CHAPTER 8

Pemba, Mozambique: Village of Joy

"God's never late; He's always on time. Even when we think He's late, He just redefines how we view time, because He works outside of it."

Love Has to Look like Something

*I*n the summer of 2014, several years after the experiences I had in chapter 1, I had the privilege to go on a mission trip to Pemba, Mozambique. I went with Iris Global, led by Heidi and Rolland Baker. I had never been on a mission trip, and I'd never flown anywhere on my own. Some of my friends recommended that I not travel to Mozambique because I had never flown anywhere on my own, but God was very clear when He told me to go to Mozambique. This was the year that God gave me a glimpse of what my purpose is. When I do something, it's all or nothing.

I was so tired of going through a cycle of disappointment and pain that I was ready to do something crazy for God; continuing to circle around in the desert for another year was no longer an option. I thought, "If I'm not living radically for Jesus, then I'm not truly living at all. No more mediocrity." I thought I knew what I was getting myself into when I went to Mozambique, but the truth is that I had no idea. As wise as it is to plan, it's often through adventure and inconvenience that our desires have a greater opportunity to become fully realized.

As my plane finally left American soil, I reminisced as I watched the places I grew up shrink smaller and smaller. I knew in my heart that everything was about to change for me forever. As I listened to the sounds of the turbo engine rumbling below me, I could hear the prophetic word spoken to me by my friend KC playing over and over again in my head: "I feel like this mission trip will reveal the reason you're alive." As this point, I knew that it wasn't going to be a once-in-a-lifetime opportunity—it was going to be the one opportunity that would set the agenda for the rest of my life.

My first stop was in Amsterdam, and because my first plane was late, it threw off all of my connecting flights to Mozambique. After landing, I immediately started running to my next connecting flight, knowing that I only had minutes to arrive at the gate. Gasping for air, I finally arrived at the front gate to my connecting flight to Johannesburg, South Africa. I showed the flight attendant my ticket, but she shook her head and said, "I'm so sorry, but you just missed that flight by about five minutes. Don't worry; you're not the only one who missed the flight. We'll reschedule your flight for free if you just head over there to the help desk."

Disappointed, I replied, "Thank you." When I got to the help desk, the clerk behind the counter asked me for my paperwork. Nervously, I handed her what I thought was everything. I'd unintentionally left out the most important paper that showed my final destination was Pemba, Mozambique. The clerk thought my final destination was Johannesburg, South Africa. I didn't think to correct her, because I was nervous, and she rescheduled me to a connecting flight that took me to Paris, France.

I had a six-hour layover in France. I really wanted to explore Paris, but I decided not to when I realized that not very many people spoke English. My smartphone was almost useless due to the fact that I hadn't planned very well for my trip. I did some shopping at the airport, grabbed a bite to eat, and talked to a few English speakers here and there. I then rested on a bench near my boarding gate. I looked at my boarding ticket, and I discovered a problem. Once I landed in Johannesburg, South Africa, I would only have about forty-five minutes to claim and recheck all of my baggage for Pemba, Mozambique. I'd need to spend the rest of my time running to the gate where my flight to Pemba would be departing. Knowing all of that and wanting to make sure I was well rested, I took a long nap before I boarded my next flight.

Once I arrived in Johannesburg, I rushed around the airport to claim my baggage and made my way to my final flight. I missed it by just a few minutes. I made my way to a help desk where I could reschedule my flight to Pemba. As I approached the front counter, I said, "Excuse me!"

The man behind the counter smiled. "Hello! How can I help you today?"

"I just missed my flight to Pemba, Mozambique, and I need to get another one. Can you help me with that?"

Enthusiastically, the man replied, "Absolutely! Can I have your ticket, please?"

After I handed him my ticket, he was quiet for about five minutes as he entered information into the computer.

Concerned, I asked, "Is everything OK?"

"Yes, sir. I'm just trying to figure this out for you."

I knew something was wrong. The man finally said, "OK, I found a flight to Pemba for you, but unfortunately the flight won't depart for another seven days."

I was shocked. "So you're saying there's no other way for me to get to Mozambique any sooner?"

"I'm so sorry, but there's no other way…Would you like to purchase these tickets?"

"No, I'm sorry."

The man behind the counter seemed surprised. "Really? Then how are you going to get to Pemba? What are you going to do?"

With a blank look on my face, I replied, "I don't know…Thank you for your time."

When I walked away from the counter, I suddenly became gripped with fear. It felt as if my heart were pounding a million beats a minute as I tried to figure out what to do next. I was in Johannesburg, South Africa, over ten thousand miles away from home. I didn't know anyone in the area I could call for help. I was extremely hungry and thirsty. I had a pounding headache, and I had to use the restroom, but the only thing I could focus on was finding a way to get to Pemba, Mozambique. I walked around the airport in a daze, an almost dreamlike state. People's voices seemed to echo, and the room started spinning for a few seconds. I kept hoping I was dreaming, but I knew I wasn't.

Then the Holy Spirit told me to relax and use the airport's thirty-minute Wi-Fi to log into social media and try to connect with Iris Global. I let Iris know that I had missed my flight to Pemba. Once my thirty minutes of free Wi-Fi ran out, I decided not to pay for additional Wi-Fi because I didn't know how much I was paying, and I also didn't know how much money I had left in my bank account. I decided to try and find someone who would be willing to convert my American dollars to South African rand so that I could make a phone call to Iris Global using the airport phone. While I was looking for someone to help me, I noticed a small candy stand right next to the airport phone. I approached and said, "Excuse me!"

One of the women turned around and smiled. "Hello! How may I help you? I'm Sheila."

"HI Sheila! So, this might sound like an unusual request, but I'm trying to call Mozambique, and I was wondering if you might be able to help me convert my US dollars to South African rand."

Sheila seemed curious. "Sure, I can help you with that. But why do you want to go to Mozambique? Nobody visits Mozambique; that's a poor country."

"Well, it's a mission trip with my church."

"Oh, OK. Well, if you want to call Mozambique, you can just use my cell phone."

Shocked, I replied, "Really? Wow, thanks!"

"No problem. You just need to purchase a thirty-minute international plan and then dial the phone number of the person you're trying to reach."

After I bought the international plan, I borrowed Sheila's cell phone and dialed the phone number of one of the Iris Global leaders, Doug. The phone rang a few times, and then Doug answered. "Hello?"

"HI! My name is Ernesto, and I'm going on a mission trip to Pemba, Mozambique, with Iris Global. Right now I'm stuck in Johannesburg because I missed my flight to Pemba, and I was told that the next flight to Pemba wouldn't be for another seven days. I was wondering if there's any way you can help me."

Doug said, "Wow, it sounds like you're in a tough situation there. I'll tell you what—I'll make some phone calls, but I can't make any promises. Right now I'm in a meeting, but call me back in three hours, and we'll go from there."

"That sounds good—thank you so much!" I said.

Sheila asked, "What happened?"

"I just finished talking with a guy named Doug, and he said he might be able to help me, but I'll need to call him back in three hours."

Sheila said, "Just in case your friend can't help you, I know another way you can get to Mozambique sooner."

I was curious. "How?"

"I know of some taxis that might be able to get you from Johannesburg to Pemba. Would you be interested in that?"

Excited, I replied, "Sure! What do I do next?"

"Well, the taxis that will take you to Mozambique aren't here at the airport. But you can take the airport taxi to the city, and you should be able to find a taxi in the city that will take you to Pemba.

Since Johannesburg is very dangerous, and you are an American, I will go with you. You can follow me."

I was surprised. "Really? Wow, thank you so much!" I followed Sheila out of the airport. Several thoughts were going through my head: "Can I really trust this person? Am I really in South Africa right now following a complete stranger out of the airport? What if she's lying and has ulterior motives? What if she's going to set me up to rob me?"

Then, almost as if she could read my mind, Sheila said, "Why do you trust me? You know that I could be lying, and I could rob you—right?"

"Well, you did let me borrow your phone, so I trust you."

Sheila smiled at that, and we continued to make our way toward the taxi. I noticed that it wasn't much of a taxi, or at least not like any taxi I'd ever seen. It was more of a shuttle bus with no doors. I had trouble getting in because my luggage was so large. Everyone on the shuttle stared at me as if I had been making a funny face; they knew I wasn't from around there. My American luggage barely fit in the shuttle, and I could tell the shuttle wasn't designed to accommodate such massive baggage.

Sheila paid for my shuttle ride, and then we took off. As we drove through the town, through stoplights, and past dirt roads where kids ran around barefoot, I knew I wasn't in the United States. The high-rise buildings and nice cars, which I would see once in a while, weren't enough to convince me that this place was anything like home. As I rode with Sheila in the shuttle, thoughts began racing through my head: "God, where is she really taking me? Will I make it to Mozambique, or will I be stuck here in Johannesburg in a hotel for seven days? Will the taxi she is taking me to actually get me to Mozambique? Then I heard the Lord say, *This is going to be a testimony that will encourage many people.*

When we finally arrived, we got off the shuttle and started walking down a dirt road. As I followed Sheila down the dirt road, it felt as if every single person stared at me as I strolled along with my massive American luggage. It also didn't help that my luggage had the word "tourist" imprinted into it. Sheila told me to follow her closely because if I ventured too far, they would rob me. As tempting as it was for me to want to stare back, I looked at no one so that I didn't attract the wrong attention.

When Sheila and I finally got to more shuttles, Sheila asked the driver how I could get to Mozambique. After a long conversation between them, Sheila told me that the shuttle would only take me to Maputo, Mozambique, which was still over a thousand miles away from Pemba. At that point, Sheila and I knew that was the wrong decision. Disappointed, we went back to the airport. When we got back, more than three hours had passed, and I remembered that Doug had told me to call him back. I asked Sheila, "Can I borrow your phone again? My friend Doug told me to call him back in three hours. He said he might be able to help me."

"Sure," she said, handing me the phone.

I dialed the phone number and Doug answered. "Hello?"

"Hi, this is Ernesto. I called you about three hours ago, and I'm stuck in Johannesburg, South Africa, and you said to call you back in three hours because you might be able to help me."

"Oh, yeah, that's right. I've got some good news for you, Ernesto! I got a hold of Will Hart, your ministry leader, and he said he'll give you a call to help you with your situation. Is this a good phone number for him to call you back at later today?"

"Well, that might be a little challenging since this is actually not my phone. My phone doesn't work in Johannesburg, and I'm borrowing this phone from a stranger at the airport."

"Oh, wow! Well, let me ask him to call you right now if that's possible. Is it OK if he gives you a call back within the hour?" I asked Sheila if that would be OK, and she nodded. "Yes, that works!" I told Doug.

About half an hour later, Will called and said, "Hey, buddy! Is this Ernesto?"

"Yup, that's me!"

Will was excited. "Well, I have some great news for you! I found out that LAM airlines has a flight to Pemba scheduled early tomorrow morning!" Relieved, I thanked him for all his help and then gave the phone back to Sheila. I thanked her for everything she had done for me and talked with her and her friend for a few minutes.

It was time to go to the LAM counter to purchase my ticket to Pemba. I grabbed my luggage to walk away, but then Sheila said, "Why are you bringing your luggage with you? That's a lot of work, and I know you are very tired. Why don't you just leave your luggage here, and we will watch it for you?" I looked at her, not knowing what to say. "You mean to tell me that after all that's happened, you still don't trust me?" I smiled, thought about it for a few seconds, and left my luggage there so that they could watch it for me as I went downstairs to purchase my plane tickets.

I purchased my plane ticket to Mozambique, then made my way back upstairs to the candy stand where Sheila and her friend were guarding my luggage. Everything was still where it was supposed to be. Once again, I thanked both of them for everything they had done for me, bought them food, and gave them some American money to keep as a souvenir. After I bought food for myself and rested for a while, Sheila and her friend helped me book a hotel room that was conveniently inside the airport. I was so exhausted that it felt like I'd been hit by a ton of bricks. I couldn't help but reflect on what God was doing not only externally but also internally. When I got to the hotel, I sat on the bed and gazed out the window, thinking to myself, "I'm here in South Africa, far away from any person I know who can help me, yet God is still taking care of me." I realized that I no longer needed to have a backup plan to bail myself out of a difficult situation in the middle of a journey He led me into.

Once I finished processing what God was doing in me, I went to bed early because I didn't want to miss my flight to Pemba. I remember setting my alarm on my phone for 5:00 a.m., but since I was so anxious about what was going to happen the next day, I woke up every hour of the night, checking my phone to make sure I didn't oversleep. I ended up waking up before my alarm clock went off. I checked out, and went to catch my final flight.

When I got to the gate, I noticed people standing in line with blue passports—American passports. Then I heard them talking about God, and I knew God was up to something. Finally, I said,

"Hello! I'm sorry to interrupt, but are you guys going to Pemba, Mozambique, with Iris Global?"

"Yeah! Are you?"

"Yes I am! I'm with Will Hart's ministry team, and I missed a couple of flights, so I'm here alone. Can I stick with you guys?"

They laughed, and someone said, "Absolutely!"

At this moment, I realized that God orchestrated everything I had recently experienced.

Even though I didn't know what to do next, God used Sheila from the Johannesburg airport, Doug from Iris Global, and Will Hart from my ministry team to find a plane ticket for me to Pemba, Mozambique, the very next day. If the story ended there, that would've been awesome enough, but God had more to reveal. Later, I found out that the flight that took me to Pemba, Mozambique, was the same flight that people from all around the world used to travel to Iris Global to begin the Harvest School of Missions. God's never late; He's always on time. Even when we think He's late, He just redefines how we view time, because He works outside of it.

Village of Joy

Once I landed in Pemba, Mozambique, with all the Harvest School students, I felt a little nervous. I remembered a conversation I had with Doug from Iris Global while I was at the Johannesburg airport. Doug had told me was that he would pick me up at the airport in Pemba. He said that he would drive me to the Iris base in his personal vehicle. Doug also told me that the airport would be small so it would be easy for me to find him. I was nervous because I didn't have any phone to contact him to make sure he was going to be there, and I didn't even know where in the airport he would be, so I figured that sticking with the Harvest School students would be the best option. After all of us finished collecting our baggage, we made our way out of the airport. A man was calling the names of all the Harvest School students to make sure everyone was present.

I walked up to the man, and I said, "Hi. I'm Ernesto, and I'm looking for a man named D—"

Doug jumped in front of him and said, "Hi, Ernesto! It's nice to finally meet you. I'm Doug, and this is my wife, Savannah. My wife is going to take you to the Iris base, so just follow her lead." I talked to Doug for a few minutes, thanked him for everything, and then followed Savannah to their vehicle, where I met the rest of Doug's family.

As we made our way to the Iris base on the bumpy dirt roads of Pemba, I looked around in amazement at what I was seeing. Pemba was obviously a place of extreme poverty, but at the same time, inexplicable joy engulfed the atmosphere. When we arrived at the Iris base, a large group of children ran up to us, smiling and waving. It felt like we were in a movie, only this was real. Prior to this moment, I didn't think it was possible for people to genuinely be that happy to see me, especially people I had never seen before in my life. That night, after connecting with my team and sharing my crazy story, Will, our team leader, took us all out to eat at a nice Mozambique restaurant.

We all followed Will to the restaurant. A little boy from the village, probably about five years old or so, looked at me, smiled, and held my hand. I didn't know where this little boy came from, and I don't even think he spoke English, but I could feel the love he had for me. He didn't have a hidden motive; he didn't want anything in return. He just wanted to hold my hand. Once we got to the restaurant, the little boy let go of my hand and walked away into the darkness of the night.

I asked Will where the little boy was going, and Will assured us that the boy knew where he was going—he was an orphan. When I realized he was an orphan, my heart sank, and my eyes welled with tears as I realized things like this are normal in Mozambique. I had never really been much of a kid person, but this experience awakened a desire inside of me that I didn't realize I had. I wanted to be a father, not only in the natural sense, but also on a spiritual level. No longer was I OK with just being proud of myself that I had started stepping into God's calling for my life; I wanted to help other people step into their callings. I wanted to really start fathering people. Later that night, after we finished eating, we went back to the Iris base to prepare for ministry the following day.

Love Births the Miraculous

On our first day of ministry, my team and I gathered together and went to preach the Gospel to the people in the local villages. During our outreach, we met a woman named Elisa who had a headache and pain on the side of her neck. After we finished praying, she told us that her headache was gone, and the pain on the side of her neck had been reduced. We prayed for her again, and God completely healed the neck pain as well. Once we finished praying, Elisa started crying because she had never encountered the love of God in this way before. Later this same day, my team and I headed back to the Iris base to feed the children.

About a thousand children showed up, and this was considered to be an average day. I helped a few of my team members pass out food. After I handed the last child his plate of beans and rice, one of my team members, Rod, walked over to me and said, "There's no more beans. There are no more beans at all! But we fed everyone; I think God must have multiplied the food!"

I said, "Wow, I think so too!" The interesting thing is that many of the children even went back for seconds, yet there was just enough for everyone.

A couple of days after this amazing experience, I thought that God had impressed me enough with what He had already done, but He wasn't finished yet. A couple of days later, it was a very special day. It was Sunday, but it wasn't just any Sunday. It was Children's Day. Children's Day only happens once a year in Mozambique, and it's like Christmas Day for all the children. On this particular day, we fed around five thousand children over a period of about four hours. Normally the children eat beans and rice, but on this day, they got foods such as fish, chicken, Coca-Cola, candy, and so on. Our job during Children's Day was to greet the children and make sure they all stayed in line while they walked into the kitchen to eat.

Many of the children would give me a high five or a handshake on their way to eat. Some of the children actually ran up to me, jumped on me, and just wanted me to hold them. I realized during those moments that we weren't just feeding children; we were giving them a love encounter with Daddy God. Later, after all the children ate, I was making my way back down to the Iris church. I noticed a man standing by a large tree. The man smiled and came to me. I didn't think anything of it until, all of a sudden, I remembered a prophetic word my friend Laura shared with me back in California before I left for Mozambique.

One of the things she prophesied was that while I was in Mozambique, I would meet a man standing underneath a large tree, and God would give me a word of knowledge for him. When I realized this was actually a divine appointment, I was excited to meet the man! The man was very excited to get to know me and learn about my background and family history. As we were talking to one another, the Holy Spirit gave me the word *father* for him. I said, "I hear the Lord giving me the word *father* for you. I feel like you have a father heart."

The man said, "Well, I am a father. I have two kids."

I smiled. "You are a great father. God is so proud of you!" After we talked a little more, we prayed over each other, hugged, and then went our separate ways. It was a great way to end such an amazing day.

On our final two days of ministry, we went to the "bush bush." This was a remote village nearby. Once we finished setting up our tents, we all gathered to watch *The Jesus Movie* with everyone from the village. After the movie was over, Heidi Baker preached. Toward the end, she said, "The same God that healed people in the movie we just watched is the same God who heals today; I believe God wants to heal people tonight!" Heidi asked all of us missionaries to create a fire tunnel. A fire tunnel is created when a very large group of us stand in a line on opposite sides of one another, forming a tunnel, to allow the people who needed healing to encounter the supernatural healing power of God.

That night, four deaf people heard, one blind man saw, people with stomach problems were completely healed, and many people who had drinking problems could no longer stand the smell of alcohol. An older man with a bad back was healed, and he accepted Christ. A person who had problems going to the bathroom was healed. Many more people accepted Christ. I had never seen so many miracles all at once.

On my final day in Pemba, while packing everything and getting ready to come back to California, the Holy Spirit reminded me of a vision God had given me while I was in the prayer hut worshiping. I believe this is a message to America.

In the vision, I saw a picture of an upside-down car, and then I saw a picture of car keys. Next, I saw nails being hammered into the ground with a hammer. People were building a spiritual bridge between Africa and the United States. Then I saw a picture of a car that was right side up. This car was a much newer car and in much better condition than the car that was upside down. The Holy Spirit told me that the car that was upside down represented the way many Americans view love—our thinking is upside down. I was trying to figure out how to use the keys to get inside of the car that was upside down, even though God wanted me to get into the new car that was right side up (a symbol of how Africans view love). The spiritual bridge between the United States and Africa was to allow the new car (love) from Africa to be able to travel to the United States and infect our country with the heart of the Father!

God is doing a new thing, and I believe the love of God is beginning to pour out in America as it is in developing countries. I believe we will see food multiplied for the homeless in America. I believe we will see the dead raised in America. I believe the good work that God started in America will be carried to completion. *Being confident of this, that he who began a good work in you will carry it on to completion until the day of Christ Jesus* (Philippians 1:6). John 3:16 doesn't say that Jesus died on the cross because He hated the world and couldn't wait to get out of here. Many of us are saying, "Oh God, take me out of this place! I hate the world; I hate the people. But I love you, Jesus, and I just want to go to heaven and be with You!" That's not quite what God had in mind for us when He sent Jesus. Regardless of our trials and tribulations, the good work Jesus began was founded on love, and the good work that He wants us to carry unto completion will be finished by stewarding love. I believe that when we learn how to love in a first-world country from a developing-world perspective, that's when the kingdom comes in a greater measure. *Blessed are the poor in spirit, for theirs is the kingdom of heaven* (Matthew 5:3).

CHAPTER 9

From Pain to Purpose

*"When you seek man's approval, you'll constantly be
searching for something you'll never obtain. But when
you live from God's approval, you'll become immersed in
a love that gives you a purpose to your pain."*

Introduction

If I never had the experiences I've had, I would never have had the desires that I have. God doesn't create pain, but He can use it to create a purpose. I feel like everything that I experienced in Mozambique taught me how to dream again. In the past, whenever people would ask me, "What do you do for a living?" my response would be, "I work for such and such." In recent years, however, I've come to an understanding that what we do for a living has nothing to do with who we work *for*. It's about who we're partnering with to bring healing and transformation into people's lives. I believe that what we do for a living is partner with Jesus in bringing the kingdom of heaven to earth in power and love.

Finishing Well

Suicide is not the answer to unanswered questions; Jesus is the answer. The work He started in you is sufficient to propel you into a purpose that will sustain you. From Scripture, King Saul was anointed to make a difference in people's lives through the authority God gave him. However, Saul allowed jealously, comparison, strife, and demonic spirits to control the way he thought about David, and in the end, he fell on his own sword (1 Chronicles 10:4). King Saul is an example of a great man of God who started his life well but ended poorly. I have struggled with suicidal thoughts many times in my past. Every time I considered suicide as a way to permanently escape the pain caused by disappointment and heartbreak, the Lord reminded me of why I'm here and what I was created for. As described back in chapter 3, the Lord told me, "If you really want to die, then die for a cause—don't die for nothing." The first thought that popped into my head was about ISIS and the Middle East.

I saw a vision of women being publically beaten, children being beheaded, and many other Christians being grossly abused because of their faith in Jesus Christ. After the Lord showed me that vision, I knew I didn't want to take my life. Since 2012, I've had a passion to partner with other believers to show the love and transforming power of Jesus to those living in the Middle East. Jesus was a carpenter, but He wasn't known for being a carpenter. He was known for healing the sick, raising the dead, loving people to the point of controversy, and dying on a cross for something He didn't deserve to give us and something we don't deserve. He gave it all to give us life more abundantly than we can fathom. I believe that one of the keys to finishing well is, as Pastor Danny Silk often says, to keep our love on in the face of fear and disappointment. After my short-term mission trip to Pemba, Mozambique, in 2014, my perspective on why God has me here has never been the same. Before going to Mozambique, my dreams revolved around who I wanted to be, but since I've gotten back from Mozambique, my dreams now revolve around who I want to build.

It is a natural God-given desire for us to want to be noticed, to feel loved, and to be known. When you seek man's approval, you'll constantly be searching for something you'll never obtain. But when you live from God's approval, you'll become immersed in a love that gives you a purpose to your pain. When there is vision, pain produces endurance, and endurance builds the foundation for the character we need to carry the weight of the promise (read Romans 5:3–4). Several years ago, when I was in my early twenties, my dreams looked much different than they do today. I used to dream about buying a big house, working for a large car dealership, buying two cars, and building a nice comfortable life for my future family. Though I had my whole life planned, something still didn't feel right about that type of lifestyle. It wasn't that I believed there was anything wrong with what I was dreaming about, but it seemed that what I dreamed about didn't give me any purpose. At that time of my life, what I really dreamed about, above anything else, was developing true covenant friendships.

I wanted people to accept me for who I was and encourage me to continue believing in the dreams God had put in my heart.

I wanted to know what it felt like to belong somewhere. The biggest problem that I had was that I didn't know why God had put me on the earth. I often felt like one out of billions of people who simply existed for no reason. While sitting in traffic on my way to work, I would glance at the people driving next to me and think, "Where exactly is everyone going? It's one thing to go to a location every day, but are any of these people actually going anywhere significant in their lives?" I felt like I was simply alive to go to work every day out of obligation, pay all my bills, go to church on Sunday, and pursue a good career path, but none of these things explained to me why in the world I existed. I wasn't satisfied with the American dream.

One thing I did know was that there was something about being intimately connected with people that made me feel a sense of belonging. There was something about sitting and talking to a friend for hours with no awareness of the time that breathed life into me. There was something that made me feel valuable when a friend would share a secret with me that he or she would never share with anyone else. There was something about helping people that made me feel like there was a greater purpose for my life than what society had taught me. I felt stuck between two realities: the abundant reality of what Scripture told me I was created for and the mundane reality that I was living in. I felt like a victim, and I felt powerless to bring heaven's reality into mine. The abundant life I wanted was one rich in relationships *with* people who would propel me to make a difference *for* people.

My whole life, up until 2010, I had suffered from borderline depression because I felt like I had no purpose. I learned a lot of good things in high school, but no one taught me how to start a revival that would change people's lives all around the world. Technical school taught me the principles I needed to know to get a good job for myself, but it never taught me how to build a legacy for others to follow for generations to come. Most of the things I needed to learn that were going to prepare me for the purpose God had planned for me didn't come from the culture I grew up in but from the Word of God I grew up believing in. Ultimately, what brought the change in my life from victim to victor wasn't more money, a better education, a better job, more fasting, or even more prophetic words. It was choosing to renew my mind.

For me, it was essential that I begin the process of renewing my mind because it was literally a matter of life and death. There have been so many times in my past that I've wanted to die simply because I didn't have a reason to live. I believe it is better to be thrown in prison for preaching the Gospel than it is to live in the prison of a purposeless mundane life. When you don't have anything worth dying for, you won't have anything to live for. But when you find something worth dying for, that's when you truly come alive. God has a divine assignment for you, but the devil also has an assignment for you. The devil's plan is to destroy you, but God's plan is for you to prosper (read John 10:10). One of the reasons I believe that so many people are negative and don't believe they can make a difference in the world is because this world is like a stream of water that flows downward. It is natural to believe what everyone else believes because many people are going in the same direction, but it takes pressure and perseverance for water to flow upstream. In fact, it is *unnatural* for water to flow upstream.

The Holy Spirit is the supernatural force that gives us the ability to swim upstream, change the direction of the water flow, heal the land, and reshape the course of history. I am all too familiar with pain and how the enemy can use it to teach us that we have no purpose. Love is an interesting thing. It's what we were created for, and it's the reason we live the way we do. Whether we thrive because of it or suffer for the sake of it, it gives us a purpose to our pain. Love cannot be prostituted. It can't be manipulated. But it can be demonstrated, because it isn't something you *feel*; it's something you *choose*. Love looks like humility, vulnerability, generosity, and tenacity, but above all, it looks like Jesus. It's the love of God, through His kindness, that leads us to repentance. In 1 Corinthians, it says that love is patient and love is *kind*, and it's the *kindness* of God that enables us to flow upstream into the glory rather than downstream into darkness (read Romans 2:4 and 1 Corinthians 13:4).

Without love, it is impossible to finish well, because love is tenacious. Tenacity is what propels you through the desert so that you're prepared to destroy the giants that stand in front of your purpose. We were all born to finish well, and when we choose to align our thoughts with that reality, heaven changes our reality.

Pain Is Temporary

For his anger lasts only a moment, but his favor lasts a lifetime; weeping may stay for the night, but rejoicing comes in the morning (Psalms 30:5). Pain is a poor teacher. It teaches us to stay away from anything that gives us even the slightest bit of discomfort. If we let pain teach us how to live our lives, we will live comfortably miserable. Anytime we do something that involves people, things will get messy, and feelings will be hurt, but the reward we will receive from the Lord for staying engaged during turmoil is always worth it. I would have never even considered holding a knife to my throat, as I talked about in chapter 3, if I knew that years later God would take me to Mozambique to show me that His love can heal blind eyes and deaf ears. I would have never considered taking my life if I knew that years later I would be part of an amazing church family at Jesus Culture. Christian speaker Christine Caine once said, "If what you see is all you see, you'll never see all there is to see."

Sometimes it's easier to quit when there's pain than it is to keep going and believe that there's a purpose to the pain. Sometimes it's easier to be disobedient and pursue a premature promise than it is to persevere through pain, tears, and sleepless nights believing in His promise in due time. Sometimes it's easier to think the desert place is our permanent place, but it's actually a temporary place that refines and prepares us for our destiny place.

In April of 2015, I experienced something really bizarre for the first time of my life. I remember drinking a cup of coffee for the first time in a long time, and afterward my entire body started itching. I eventually went to bed, but I couldn't sleep. I felt anxious, excited, frustrated, and sad all at the same time. I believe I may have had some type of allergic reaction to the coffee, but what started as an allergic reaction turned into a spiritual attack. As the days went by, the itchy feeling went away, but I felt drained and exhausted all the time. Since I thought I wasn't getting enough sleep, I tried getting a full eight hours of sleep for several nights in a row, but that didn't change anything. I then thought that I was getting too much sleep, because I knew that too much sleep had made me feel lazy in the past, so I tried sleeping less, but that didn't help either. In an attempt to remedy the situation, I tried exercising more and changing my diet, but still no difference.

The last thing I tried was going to the doctor, but after spending several hundreds of dollars and checking out perfectly fine, I still felt weak and tired all day, every day. The only thing my doctor recommended was a pill for vertigo, but I decided not to take them because of the side effects—"possible feelings of fatigue." I continued to feel weak and tired for about two and a half months. Though I continued to function as normal, it greatly affected my mood. I got headaches often. I had to drink much more water than usual, and I would get dizzy spells from time to time without any explanation. During that two and a half months, I became very depressed. Negative things I normally wouldn't think about became forerunners in my thoughts. God's truth became very fuzzy, and the facts of life stuck out like a sore thumb. In my head, I was hearing demonic voices trying to explain the reason for my circumstances: *You will never have your own family because there's something wrong with you. You will die alone because nobody cares about you. Nothing will ever change so you might as well give up.*

What sustained me were my brothers and sisters in Christ, who kept me in prayer along the way, listening to prophetic words, reading the Bible, and spending more personal time with the Lord in prayer than usual. As crazy as it sounds, I felt as if I was slowly dying. I didn't understand why I was experiencing these things, but I continued to persevere and trust that God would work it out for good (read Romans 8:28). Then finally, after two and a half months, the Lord healed me. I was so discouraged, because I had planned to go back to Mozambique around that period of time, but circumstances prevented it from happening. After the Lord healed me, I started spending some time asking Him whether or not I was supposed to go back to Mozambique. The Lord said, *Yes, but if you had gone back to Mozambique now, you wouldn't have been physically able to handle the harsh conditions. I want you to be fully prepared when you go back to Mozambique. I love you too much to let you go back in this condition.*

I was surprised when the Lord told me that, because I had never thought about things that way. I could clearly remember how harsh the living conditions had been in Mozambique in 2014. I don't believe that God caused something bad to happen to prevent me from going to Mozambique in 2015. But I do believe that He used the bad that happened to me to prepare me for the destiny that He is planning for me. Sometimes it feels like there is no end to the dark tunnel. Sometimes darkness appears brighter than light in itself. Sometimes it's easier to give up than it is to keep believing that there is a purpose to the pain. There are two different worlds that we live in simultaneously. One is tangible, and another is intangible. What we choose to believe about ourselves must not align with what is seen, because what is tangible is temporary, but what is unseen lasts forever.

Pain is temporary, but the joy that comes in the morning is the same joy that propels us through the mourning. Joy is supernatural by nature. It isn't defined by how we feel; it's defined by how *He* feels. I believe joy is like an electrical current. For those unfamiliar with how electricity works, voltage pushes a current through resistance in order to power electronic devices. Voltage is the power of the Holy Spirit, joy is the current, and resistance is the pain that we experience in this life. Without the Holy Spirit pushing, there is no joy to carry us through the resistance. One of the reasons many people live in defeat is because they don't know the joy of the Lord and how to let it strengthen them as they walk through pain. A current without voltage cannot make it through the resistance to power an electronic device. Similarly, striving to push through pain in the natural world is impossible without the joy of the Lord, which is supernatural. Just as electricity travels faster than the speed of sound, the Lord can take us out of our pain and into our purpose just as fast, as long as we don't give up. It isn't what you see that becomes your reality; it's what you choose to believe about what you see that will determine your destiny.

CHAPTER 10

Love Never Gives Up: A Marriage Testimony

"Hope deferred makes the heart sick, but a longing fulfilled is a tree of life."

Proverbs 13:12

Part I: Boy Meets Girl

Daniel and Christina are two amazing friends of mine who love the hell out of people for a living. As of this writing, they've been happily married for four years. I believe their lives are a great example of what the normal Christian life should look like, but it didn't start off that way. Throughout their years of pain, hardship, and disappointment, they have chosen to keep their love going regardless of what life throws at them. This is their story.

Meet Daniel

My friend Daniel was born in Melbourne, Australia. Since the day he was born, his mother knew that he had the great call of God in his life. God had blessed him with the gift of healing. One Saturday morning, Daniel's mom was suffering from a migraine. Daniel, only two years old, walked up to his mother and laid his hands on her head while saying, "Praise the Lord, praise the Lord!" His mother was instantly healed. At that moment, Daniel's mother knew that God had given Daniel a gift to bring healing and restoration into people's lives. Another day, when Daniel was three years old, God sent an angel into Daniel's room to tell him about the Gospel of Jesus Christ. Daniel's mother knew that God had a big plan for him, but the devil had a plan also. During Daniel's teenage years, he wandered off and became a drug addict. After four years of drug abuse, he eventually began suffering from what seemed to be a mental illness. One night, Daniel's mom was praying for him. Jesus walked into Daniel's room, kissed him on the forehead, and set him completely free from drug addiction. Daniel was twenty-one years old at the time. As a side note, Jesus had never stopped pursuing Daniel because His love never gives up. The fact that God pursues us is what makes Christianity different from other religions. I once heard evangelist Reinhard Bonnke say, "In other religions, man pursues God, but in Christianity, God pursues man." Shortly after Daniel was set free from drug addiction, he started volunteering with Youth for Christ and other various ministries.

While serving in a local ministry, Daniel got involved with a house church and met a missionary named Chris who traveled often to the Philippines for mission work. Daniel became very intrigued with missions. After being connected with Chris for some time, he went on a mission trip with Chris to the Philippines for a few weeks. While they were in the Philippines, they preached the Gospel in the mountains and everywhere else God led them. After getting back from the Philippines, Daniel continued to serve in local ministries. After being back in Australia for some time, he knew he was supposed to go back to the Philippines. When his grandmother gave him his inheritance before she passed away, he used some of that money to plan another trip to the Philippines on his own.

For Daniel's second trip to the Philippines, he planned to stay in Manila with a friend named Jerry whom he'd connected with the first time he traveled there. But when he finally arrived in Manila, he got into a taxi, went to his hotel room, and immediately curled into the fetal position. He asked himself, "What the heck am I doing here?" It was at that moment that Daniel processed the reality of his situation. Not only did he know that Manila was one of the most dangerous parts of the Philippines, but he also knew that his friend Jerry wasn't even going to be in the Philippines for the first week Daniel was there. The next morning, the local Filipino ministry team picked Daniel up from his hotel room. Daniel was taken to his slum where he would be staying for the next seven weeks.

While Daniel was in the slum, he spent a lot of time processing with God about everything that was happening to him. Not long after, Bayani, a man from the local Filipino leadership team, went to visit Daniel. "Hey, Daniel! How's everything going so far?" he asked.

Daniel said, "I'm doing great. I've been spending time with the Lord, and I'm excited about what God's about to do through us!"

Bayani was excited. "I'm glad you're here! Well, the reason I'm here is because I would like to invite you to preach at our church this Sunday. How does that sound?"

Enthusiastically, Daniel said, "Sure, I would be honored!" After a few days, Daniel suddenly felt afraid. Even though he'd been in the Philippines before, he was gripped with fear because of his circumstances. As Daniel continued to seek the Lord during this difficult time, he received a breakthrough one day before he preached. Daniel was experiencing the perfect love of God that casts out fear.

It was Sunday. Daniel was excited to see what God was about to do. During the church meeting that Daniel preached at, the first person who walked to the front for prayer fell to the ground as soon as Daniel laid hands on him. People started shaking and manifesting under the anointing of the Holy Spirit. That Sunday, God not only brought healing and restoration to the people Daniel preached to, but He also brought a deeper level of revelation to Daniel regarding his calling. During the rest of Daniel's stay in the Philippines doing ministry with his friend Jerry, Jesus revealed to Daniel in many ways that miracles flow from intimacy with the Father.

After he got back to Australia, he connected again with his friends and ministry partners—Chris and his wife, Samantha. While at their home, Daniel noticed a book on the shelf: *When Heaven Invades Earth*, by Bill Johnson. Intrigued, Daniel said to Chris, "Hey, man, this book looks really good—can I borrow it?"

Chris glanced at the book, and then said, "No, unfortunately you can't, because my wife and I are getting ready to go on a four- to five-month mission trip to Asia, and we feel like we need to bring that book with us. Sorry, bro."

Disappointed, Daniel replied, "I completely understand. Just thought I'd ask!" Later that same week, Daniel's mother, Regina, felt the Lord tell her to go to the Christian bookstore and buy a book for Daniel during her lunch break. Regina wrapped the book in a brown paper bag and put it on her kitchen table.

She called Daniel and said, "Hey, Daniel! So I went to the bookstore earlier this week, and I saw this book, and the Lord told me to buy it for you. You should stop by and pick it up whenever you're free!"

"I'm on the way!" When Daniel arrived at his parents' house, he rang the doorbell.

Regina opened the door holding the book wrapped in the brown paper bag and said, "Hey, Daniel! How are you? Well, here's the book I was telling you about. I hope you like it!" When Daniel opened the bag, he was pleasantly surprised by the title of the book: *When Heaven Invades Earth*, by Bill Johnson. He now knew that God wanted him to read that book. Months later, the Lord told Daniel to go back to the Philippines for another two weeks to connect with Chris and Samantha. During that mission trip, Daniel gave words of knowledge from the pulpit for the first time. Each time he went to the Philippines, God increased his anointing to heal the sick.

When Daniel got back to Australia, he started doing street ministry and saw people get healed instantly from various physical ailments. He was so hungry for the presence of God that he was ready and willing to do whatever God said, no matter the cost. The passion Daniel had for the Lord eventually led him to the spirit-filled Stairway Church, where he connected with other believers who had the same passion for Jesus. One Sunday evening, he attended an evening service at Stairway Church. After the service ended, Daniel's friend Randy came to him and said, "Hey, Daniel!

So a bunch of us from church are going to McDonald's to hang out. Wanna come?"

It was a tough decision for Daniel because he knew that he had to start work at six thirty the next morning. But he made the sacrifice because he knew it would be great to meet new people and make new friends. After thinking about it for a second, Daniel replied, "Sure!"

On a very important side note, while Daniel knew he had been called to demonstrate the kingdom of God, he also knew that he had been called to be a husband. At this point in his life, Daniel had been single for seven years. During those years, he had dated a woman named Susan for a month. They had been friends for some time. But the confusion of whether they would just remain friends or become more than friends left him with all kinds of tormenting thoughts. Susan had a heart for the Lord, she wanted to do missionary work, and she wanted kids—all traits that Daniel wanted in a future wife. But because of all the oppression brought on by their confusing relationship, Daniel knew she wasn't the woman he was supposed to marry.

On Daniel's drive to McDonald's, he started thinking about his future wife. The Lord reminded him of a prophetic word he had received from a man who attended Daniel's mother's church. He remembered that man's words as though it were yesterday: "Time and space are of no relevance to God. If you're called to be a husband to someone, you can be a husband to her in prayer right now." By this point in Daniel's life, he had been praying for his future wife's needs for some time. He was looking forward to meeting some new friends at McDonald's, but God had something there that was much better than Daniel could ever dream of.

Meet Christina

Christina grew up on the beautiful island of Oahu, Hawaii. She was the oldest child and had four younger brothers. She had known Jesus for as long as she could remember. Her grandmother took her to church, and life seemed to be going well for Christina, but when she turned eight years old, things changed. Her family started their own business. The demands of the business made everyone very busy. The stress took a toll on her family. They no longer had time for the things they used to do together. When they stopped going to church, Christina knew something was wrong, and she felt empty and heartbroken. She questioned her faith in God. Eventually, she decided that it was easier to be an atheist than it was to believe in something that didn't seem to fix the brokenness in her heart. During her teenage years, Christina developed a passion for surfing. As she connected with other surfers, she was introduced to drugs and the Hawaiian party scene.

Christina dated different men, but none of the relationships were honorable. The men in her relationships were abusive, controlling, manipulative, and deceitful, and her heart was broken time and time again. After years of the abuse, she developed a mistrust of men.

Many years later, after having her heart broken so many times, Christina went back to church. She left her old life behind and fully committed herself to God. At church, the Lord healed Christina's heart. She became aware of her heart's desires. One of those desires was to be a wife someday, so she bought a promise ring. She brought it before her entire church to publically declare that she was going to wait for her future husband.

Sometime later, a prophet from New Zealand told Christina that she had a heart like Heidi Baker. He told her that she was going to go to Mozambique in Africa. Later on, Christina's friend told her that Heidi Baker was going to be in town for three days for a conference. Yet her friend had told her this without knowing that Christina had already gotten a prophetic word about Heidi Baker. Christina knew that she was supposed to go to that conference. At the conference, Christina received the confirmation she needed to go to Mozambique. She planned to attend the Harvest School of Missions.

While traveling there, Christina realized that she didn't have enough money to cover all of her expenses, but God provided miraculously. When she was on the plane, a stranger overheard Christina talking about Mozambique and gave her a large sum of money for her trip. Once Christina arrived, she knew that she still didn't have enough money to cover all her expenses, and a man behind her gave her money toward her trip. God used two complete strangers to give Christina a total of about $400, which was enough money to pay for all of her luggage fees and expenses.

But God completely amazed Christina during her time in Mozambique. She shared a house with ten girls and really learned about the Father's heart. While in the bush in Mozambique, Christina, along with her team, watched a person who was blind in the right eye get healed. The eye went from white to brown to black, and then the person's vision was restored!

During Christina's time in Mozambique, God was not only using her to work miracles. He also performed miracles in her by healing her dyslexia and her broken heart. Christina experienced firsthand that God can do anything. She graduated the Harvest School. One of the women she had shared a house with, Elizabeth, was from Melbourne, Australia. They instantly became like sisters, and Elizabeth told Christina that she should pray about visiting her in Australia sometime.

From that time, Christina received at least eight prophetic words about going to Australia. She had about $200 in her bank account, and she stayed with a family in Mozambique for two months after graduating the Harvest School. But then God woke Christina up one morning and told her that it was time to go to Australia. He told her that she was to apply for a master's program in development. Out of obedience, Christina applied for the Australian master's program, and she got accepted. The tuition was $40,000. Not too long after, Christina got her tax return, which was about $2,000, and that was just enough money to book a one-way flight to Australia. Elizabeth told her that it would be a great experience for Christina to serve for an NGO (a nonprofit organization that houses troubled and abused teenagers) when she got to Australia. Christina agreed that serving for an Australian NGO would be a great experience for her to show troubled teens the love of God.

Christina showed up in Australia with only $30. While serving at the NGO, she had the privilege of living there for free while she worked as a house mom. But eventually she moved in with Elizabeth. When Christina moved in with Elizabeth, they were both so broke that they were mainly eating carrots because they didn't have any money.

God told her that she was to go to Melbourne University, but Christina felt really insecure because it was the number-one university in all of Australia. But Melbourne University accepted her application, and they also credited her a full semester because of her time in Africa. That saved her about $20,000 on her tuition.

Christina had gotten to the point in her life in which she was seeing demonstrations of the goodness of God in almost every way, shape, and form. After about a month of being in Melbourne, Christina and Elizabeth went to McDonald's after church one night to grab a bite to eat. Little did she know, God had something much better than a Happy Meal planned for her at McDonald's.

Part II: A Match Made in Heaven

Daniel finally arrived at McDonald's. Before he got to the front door, he glanced to the right and saw his friend Elizabeth from church. She was walking into McDonald's front entrance. All of a sudden, he noticed another woman getting out of Elizabeth's car, and she sparked his interest. As she started walking toward the McDonald's, Daniel looked at her and thought, "Whoa! Who's that? I didn't see her at church!" When she finally got to the entrance, Daniel opened the door for her and said, "Hi! Were you at Stairway Church earlier, by any chance?"

The women replied, "Yes, I was!"

Daniel extended his hand toward her. "Hi! I'm Daniel."

They shook hands. "Hi, Daniel! I'm Christina." They ate together with the rest of their friends from church. After about ten minutes of fellowship, Daniel and Christina were talking exclusively with one another. Their conversation was so riveting that they talked for two to three hours about Jesus and what He had done for them in their lives. They were naturally drawn to each other.

After almost three hours of conversation, Daniel looked at his watch. It was almost midnight. Surprised, he said, "Wow! Did you know we've been talking for almost three hours?"

"Really? I didn't even notice!"

"I'm so sorry, but I've got to go because I have to work at six thirty tomorrow morning. It was great to meet you, Christina. I'm looking forward to connecting with you guys again soon!"

"Same here; have a great night!" Christina said.

Daniel said good-bye to everyone, got in his car, and headed home. He thought, "Why didn't I get her number? She sure is an amazing woman. I feel like there's something different about her." He thought about Christina from that night on.

A week later, Daniel was at church. He looked for Christina to see how she was doing. When he found her, Christina said, "Hey! I'm glad you're here, because there's a man who wants me to pray for him, but I don't pray for guys alone."

"Cool! I'll pray with you," Daniel said.

After the service ended, Elizabeth came over. "Hey, guys! So a bunch of friends and I are going to McDonald's again tonight. Wanna come with us?"

Daniel and Christina looked at each other, and he replied, "Sure, that sounds good!"

Christina asked, "Can I get a ride with you?"

"Sure!" Daniel was excited. Christina seemed to have gotten to a point in which she felt safe with him.

That night at McDonald's, they exchanged phone numbers. Christina knew there was something different about Daniel. She was normally very guarded around men, with good reason, but she knew she could trust Daniel. From that point on, Daniel, Christina, and Elizabeth were inseparable. Although Daniel and Christina were just friends, he was really developing romantic feelings for her. He thought she was beautiful, intelligent, Spirit filled, and everything he was looking for in a future wife. He knew he was falling in love with her.

The next day, Christina was at home doing some chores. While doing laundry, she became frustrated and overwhelmed when her washing machine broke. It seemed like everything around her house was falling apart. She eventually took a short break and sat on the couch to process everything she was feeling. She found herself thinking about Daniel. She remembered that he lived five minutes away. Maybe he was available to help her and Elizabeth with their chores.

Excited, Christina went into the kitchen where Elizabeth was doing dishes. "Hey! So I was just thinking—lately we've been so overwhelmed with all the chores and things that need to be fixed around here that it seriously feels like everything is falling apart. Do you remember Daniel, from church?"

Elizabeth replied, "Of course I do. You guys talked for, like, three hours that one night at McDonald's. How could I forget something epic like that?"

Christina smiled. "I know, right? That was an awesome night! Well, since Daniel only lives about five minutes away, we should have him come over to help with all this stuff we need to fix around here. What do you think?"

Excited, Elizabeth replied, "Yeah, that sounds like a great idea! You should text him and see what he thinks."

"That's perfect," said Christina. "Thanks!"

Later that day, Christina sent a text message to Daniel: "Hey, Daniel! This is Christina from McDonald's the other night. How are you? I was just wondering if you might be free sometime this week to help my roommate and me fix and clean up some things around our house. We've been super overwhelmed with everything that needs to be done, and I thought since you live so close to us, it would also be great for us to catch up! Hope you're enjoying your day!"

Twenty minutes later, Daniel sent a text back. "Oh hey, Christina! I'm doing great. Just got finished running some errands around the house, and now I'm prepping for dinner. Yeah, I'd love to help you guys out sometime. That'd be cool! Let me know what day sounds good to you, and I'll check my schedule." Christina was growing fond of Daniel.

A few days later, on Monday morning, Christina woke up early to do some journaling and soaking with God. God told her to write about the cost of being a disciple. She heard the Lord tell her, "It's not going to be like Avon, but you'll know." Christina didn't understand what that meant, but that's what she heard. After she finished, she and Elizabeth sat down to breakfast. While at the table talking, Elizabeth smiled and said, "You know what?"

"What?"

"We should go to the beach!"

Christina's eyes widened. She smiled and said, "Yeah! We should totally do that. The weather is amazing today!"

They went to the beach and spent most of their morning enjoying the sun, the waves, and good conversation. The beach was Christina's happy place because it reminded her of Hawaii.

Later that morning, Daniel called Christina to see what she and Elizabeth were up to. "Hey, Daniel! How are ya?"

"I'm great! I was spending some time with the Lord today and just wanted to give you guys a call to see what's up."

"That so awesome! Yeah, Elizabeth and I are just chillin' at the beach."

"Really? You know, I'm not too far away from there."

"Well, you should join us then!"

Excited, Daniel replied, "I'll see you there in a bit!"

The three of them enjoyed the beach and the fellowship. About half an hour into their conversation, Elizabeth looked down at her watch. She realized that she had almost forgotten about some errands she had to run in the city. Elizabeth cut off Daniel in the middle of his conversation and said, "Hey, Daniel! I'm so sorry, but I need to go now; I have some things I need to do in the city. Could you bring Christina home later?"

Daniel replied, "Sure, I'd love to."

Later that day, Daniel and Christina walked to his car. "How are you feeling?" Daniel asked.

Christina laughed. "My heart is so happy! I just love the beach, and I processed so much with the Lord today!"

"That's awesome! Well, I asked because I want to invite you to lunch tomorrow with my friends Bob and Helen. I think you guys would have a lot in common."

Excited and filled with anticipation, Christina replied, "Sure, that sounds great!"

Daniel drove Christina home, went back to his apartment, and went to bed. The next day, they went to Bob and Helen's house. Once inside, Bob showed them to the family room table.

Daniel introduced Christina, and they all started talking. Christina looked at him and said, "We should pray for them!"

Daniel smiled and replied, "Sure!"

Christina started prophesying over Helen. "I see you as this open rose…"

As Daniel listened, he was reminded of a prophetic word he had given Helen only a month prior. Before he'd even met Christina, he had told Helen, "I see this closed rose, but I see the Lord opening you up and you blooming." Daniel realized that he and Christina's prophetic words to Helen were almost identical. After eating, Daniel and Christina said their good-byes. Helen remembered Daniel's almost identical prophetic word from a month prior. She smiled and said to her husband, Bob, "Wow. Now there's a match made in heaven."

Daniel and Christina enjoyed the rest of their afternoon together. He felt it was time for him to express how he felt. That evening, he took Christina out to eat. During dinner, he said, "I hate this."

Confused, Christina asked, "You hate what?"

"I hate having crushes."

She was still oblivious. "Who do you have a crush on?"

"Hello?" Daniel said, trying to make his point.

"Oh…" Christina had finally figured out what was going on—Daniel had a crush on her.

After a few seconds of processing, she said, "Well, this is pretty awkward, because I have this list."

"OK, well, I have a list too."

Christina was curious. "Well, what's on your list?"

"My wife's going to be strong, kind, compassionate, prophetic, and loving. What's on your list?"

"Tall, blond, South African, diplomat, surfer, and guitarist." Christina hadn't yet realized that her list was more of a defense mechanism than it was of features she wanted in a future husband. She laughed. "You know, my list seems really superficial!"

Daniel was a gentleman and chose not to reply, and Christina noticed. She explained to Daniel why a relationship would never work between them.

After dinner, they went back to the city. During the drive, he said to her, "Well, whatever happens, we're still going to be friends." She looked at him and smiled. Hearing Daniel say that was comforting for her because regardless of what happened, she knew she wasn't going to lose a friend.

Daniel was disappointed. Even though he knew they would still be friends, he was saddened that she didn't give him the opportunity to pursue her heart. But he was still filled with the peace of the Lord, which surpassed understanding. He went home and went to bed.

The following morning, Daniel called his friend Bob, from the previous night. "Dude, I told her how I felt about her, and she didn't feel the same."

Bob disagreed. "No, no—I feel peace about this!"

"Dude, get the memo. She said no. It's not happening."

Bob insisted, saying, "No, I feel peace. God's gonna do something!"

"OK, whatever."

A few days later, Christina was processing everything that had happened. While she was spending time with the Lord, she heard a voice say very clearly, "Date Daniel." Christina wasn't sure where the voice came from, and she immediately rebuked it.

Confused, Christina said to the spirit, "I rebuke you, satan!"

Christina heard it again. "Date Daniel."

At that point, she wasn't just confused—she was afraid. She didn't know what to do. She told Elizabeth. "Elizabeth, I'm hearing voices! I'm hearing this voice telling me to date Daniel."

Elizabeth was confused. "I thought you didn't like him."

Christina replied, "I don't! Not like *that*." They decided to intercede in prayer and come against the voices. Finally, Christina said, "I need to go back to my room… I need to pray more." Once in her room, she heard the Lord tell her to read from her journal. She suddenly remembered what God said to her the morning before Daniel expressed his feelings. She watched it in her mind as if it were a movie:

It was Monday morning. Christina thought it was a good morning to spend some time in the presence of the Lord. While she was soaking with

*God, He reminded her of prophetic words that someone gave her in 2008—
"It's not going to be like Avon."*

"I know what that means—an Avon sales representative,"
Christina thought. The Lord was telling her that a disciple isn't like an
Avon representative that comes to the door uninvited. It was going to
be a person she knew. Christina wasn't sure she understood what that
meant, but that's what she had heard. She remembered that a couple
of days after she had rejected Daniel, she went to an Avon multilevel-
marketing meeting with a friend who was also an Avon representative:

*Christina arrived at the meeting with Cara. She thought about how, on
that prior Monday morning, God had told her something about Avon. While
she sat in the Avon meeting, the words kept playing in her head. "It's going
to be someone you'll know." Then the Lord said to Christina, "She's going to
confirm what I'm saying to you." Later that night, Christina went to dinner
with Cara. They were chatting away, when all of a sudden, seemingly out of
nowhere, Cara looked at her dead in the eyes and said, "You know."*

Christina didn't know how to process these memories. She
was afraid and confused at the same time. But she trusted God
to give her more insight regarding the voice that told her to date
Daniel. God continued to replay the same memories and visions in
her head. She kept hearing a voice saying, "It's going to be someone
you'll know." Christina got another vision of her friend Cara looking at her dead in the eyes and saying, "You know…"

She finally realized that the voice was God's. For a while,
she was in denial because she was afraid to trust again, but the
Lord confirmed to her that Daniel was trustworthy. The reason
Christina wanted so much confirmation regarding her relationship

with Daniel was because Christina didn't want to just date for fun. She knew that if she were going to date Daniel, he would be the man she would marry.

Although the Lord had already told Christina that Daniel was the man she was going to marry, God continued to give her more confirmation. The Lord directed her to read something very specific in another one of her journals. She had written it down a long time ago. Once she found the specific entry, it read, "a husband in Australia." She was shocked yet amazed at how much confirmation God was giving her. She ran to Elizabeth and said, "Hey! There's something really crazy and amazing that I want you to read!"

Elizabeth read the journal entry. "Are you joking?"

Christina was excited. "No! Isn't that interesting?"

"You know what? Honestly, I feel peace about this whole thing. Actually, I really like him, and I think you guys would be awesome together!"

Shocked, Christina smiled and said, "Why didn't you tell me this?"

Elizabeth shrugged and said, "I don't know." Now that Elizabeth also approved of Daniel, Christina had a wake-up call. She hadn't just received more confirmation about Daniel being the right man for her—she had received an awakening to love. Christina was falling in love with Daniel.

Later in the week, on Thursday, Christina sent a text to Daniel. "Can you call?"

Daniel replied, "Sure." He was on his way to his sister Rebecca's house. When Daniel finally pulled up to his sister's driveway, he turned off his engine and dialed Christina's number.

"Hey! How are you?" Christina said.

"I'm good. How are you? What's up?"

They talked for an hour and a half. Christina knew she had to tell Daniel what God had revealed to her about him. But she was very nervous because she wasn't sure how he would respond, since she'd rejected him earlier that week. When Christina was finally ready to share, she got very quiet. She then danced around the topic as much as possible. Finally, she said nervously, "So... um...just between friends, I've never been taken out on a real date before...OK, bye!" She hung up.

Daniel was very confused. He called her back and asked, "What does that mean?"

Still nervous, she replied, "All right, well...I think we should hang out this Saturday evening. How does that sound?"

"Sure, that would work." Daniel wasn't sure what was happening. He wondered, "Is Saturday going to be a date or just a hangout between friends?" Meanwhile, Rebecca was wondering why he had been sitting in his car in her driveway for an hour and a half. She opened the front door to check on him.

Daniel got out of his car and walked into Rebecca's house while scratching his head. He said, "There's this awesome woman I've been friends with for some time now, and earlier this week I told her that I really liked her, but she rejected me. Then just now, in your driveway, I called her, and she told me that she's never been on a real date before, and she wants to hang out with me on Saturday. I don't know if she wants to hang out as friends or if we're going on a date...What do think that means?"

Perplexed, Rebecca said, "I have no idea what that means."

"I need to go home and pray about this." Daniel gave his sister a hug and then drove home to spend time in prayer with the Lord.

While praying and worshipping God, Daniel was hit with both the fire and joy of the Lord simultaneously. During his time with the Lord, Daniel wasn't able to talk for about half an hour. The Lord ministered to Daniel during that time while preparing him for what was coming next.

Friday evening, Daniel and Christina talked more about Saturday over the phone. During that conversation, she finally said, "OK, God told me to date you." Everything changed at that moment. Now they were more than friends. They both agreed that they were going to go on a date.

The next day, Daniel woke up fully aware that he was about to go on a date with Christina. One of the first things Daniel read was the proverb of the day, from 13:12. *Hope deferred makes the heart sick, but a longing fulfilled is a tree of life.* After spending time with the Lord, he decided to buy roses for Christina. All the roses in the store looked generic, but there was one bouquet that stood out to him. They were very unique; they looked as if they were on fire. Daniel thought of them as "flaming roses." After buying them, Daniel thought, "Wait a minute. This whole time, Christina and I have been friends. Now that we're dating, it's going to be weird for Elizabeth if I show up at their house with flowers for Christina." He sent a text to Christina: "Is Elizabeth there? 'Cause I bought you something."

Christina wrote back, "What did you buy me? Oh, that's OK, 'cause I know you have surprises planned." Daniel suddenly remembered that he had told Christina that he was going to surprise her for their date. He had forgotten, and he had absolutely nothing planned.

He ran around like a mad man, calling restaurants and trying to figure out what they were going to do on their date. Meanwhile, Christina was also very nervous. This was her first *real* date. She wanted to look her best so she bought a special outfit.

That day, Daniel prayed about his relationship with Christina. He didn't want to sacrifice the call of God in his life for just another relationship. But if it was the *right* relationship that would unite them and complement both their callings, he would proceed. Daniel asked God if this was really His will. The Lord said to Daniel, *Go and enjoy yourself.* Daniel knew he had the green light, so he got in his car and drove to pick up Christina for their date. At the restaurant, they couldn't even focus on eating because they both felt the glory of God blessing their conversation and their relationship.

After they'd been talking for a while, Christina said, "I don't date anyone except for my husband."

"I don't date anyone except for my wife."

"I do things quickly," she said.

"So do I."

A week later, they started planning financially for their wedding. Everyone thought they'd known each other for years, but they'd only known each other for a little over a month. They felt the Lord telling them to have their wedding in Hawaii with Christina's family. After two weeks of dating, they went to Daniel's parents' house so that Christina could meet his parents for the first time. Daniel's mom, Regina, and Christina left the room to talk privately. Daniel's father, Justin, looked at him and said, "This is going to be a really quick courtship, isn't it?"

"Yup," Daniel said.

"You know, Daniel, marriage is a serious thing, but you know that. What God has brought together, let no man tear apart. Not many people can say that God's brought them together." Hearing this, Daniel told his mother that he and Christina had been talking about weddings.

Surprised, Regina said, "You don't talk about weddings, because there hasn't been a proposal! You haven't even asked for Christina's father's permission—you need to do that. I'm going to go, and you need to sort that out." She left the room.

Christina immediately pulled out her cell phone to call her father. Daniel was anxious, as he had never spoken to Christina's parents, but he knew this was necessary. Christina said, "Hi, Daddy! It's Christina. I've got Daniel here, and he wants to ask for your permission to marry me." She handed Daniel the phone.

Daniel was so unprepared that it seemed as if the phone were coming to him in slow motion. Christina's father gave his permission, but her mother was also listening to their conversation. She said, "This is totally God! This is awesome! Yeah, of course! You know, you also need to call Christina's grandfather and ask for his permission as well."

Christina's grandfather lived on the same street as her parents. The word spread within minutes that Christina was getting married. Daniel called her grandfather. "Hello, Gary."

"You can call me Grandpa," Gary said. He knew why Daniel was calling.

"All right. Well, I'm calling because I'm asking for permission to marry your granddaughter. She's amazing, has a heart for the Lord, and I'm looking forward to being a part of this family."

"You're already a part of the family—welcome!"

Daniel hung up and noticed that Christina was crying. She took off her promise ring and handed it to him. As he held the ring, he looked Christina in the eyes and said, "Christina, will you marry me?"

With tears in her eyes, she responded, "Yes, I will!"

He slipped the ring on her finger as a symbol of their engagement. (Later, Daniel bought her an actual wedding ring, but at that moment, the promise ring was all they needed to solidify their engagement.)

Regina knocked on the door. "Well, is it done?"

"Yeah, were engaged!"

Filled with joy, Regina hugged Christina while shouting, "Oh my goodness! Now I can call you my daughter-in-law!"

Within a few days after they were engaged, God provided the money to cover many things: their plane tickets to Hawaii, Christina's wedding dress, Christina's wedding shoes, and so on. Shortly after, they went to premarriage counseling. They received and heeded the advice that was given to them.

Finally, Daniel and Christina flew out to Hawaii to get married in 2012. Afterward, they went back to Australia and moved into Daniel's apartment. About four months after they got married, they both stopped and realized the reality of their situation. Daniel was still working full time, and Christina was still in school doing her master's program in development while working a part-time job. Needless to say, they both had a lot on their plates.

Trust without Borders

Shortly after they'd moved back to Australia, Christina met with Daniel's grandmother one afternoon for tea. His grandmother said, "I feel like I'm supposed to pay for you and Daniel to go to Hawaii for Christmas."

"Wow! I don't know what else to say other than…thank you so much!" Excited, she drove home and told Daniel. They both knew that God wanted them to travel to Hawaii by Christmastime. Meanwhile, Christina received an internship through school to go anywhere in the world and work with a nongovernmental organization (NGO). She needed to do this in order to graduate. They realized that Christina could serve for two months and complete her school assignment in time for both of them to travel to Hawaii by Christmas. The only problem was that after her time with the NGO, Christina would only have about six weeks to finish writing a seventy-five-page report before graduating and traveling to Hawaii. But they trusted that God had them covered, so they packed everything and went to Uganda.

While there, Daniel preached the Gospel in small mountain churches, and Christina worked full time for her internship in Kampala. Daniel felt the Lord saying they needed to move to the West Coast of the United States, and he shared this with Christina. But they agreed that they needed more confirmation about this.

They went back to Australia after the two months were complete. Most people would not be able to leave their job for two months, do missionary work, and expect that they could work at the same job, but Daniel went back to work at the same job because of the favor God had given him there. After settling back in, Christina realized that she only had five weeks left to finish her seventy-five-page report for her master's program. During that same week, Christina launched a petition to help Daniel immigrate to the United States. They were both incredibly stressed out, so they prayed about the situation just to make sure that it was really God's will.

Later that same week, they went to Stairway Church. The Lord spoke to Christina and reminded her about moving to the West Coast. Although they both knew Hawaii wasn't quite the West Coast, they knew that going there was their first step. While Christina knew that they'd move to America, she didn't know the procedure or the steps to take. She asked God what to do first. God told her to call hotlines and obtain more information on how to complete Daniel's petition to become an American resident. She followed His instructions.

After several days of calling and receiving very little information, she spoke with a nice southern woman named Charlotte. Christina immediately felt peace about this woman, as if God were up to something. Christina asked, "What do you recommend we do? How would you navigate my type of scenario? I'm trying to go through the second step to petition for my husband to become an American resident, but we only have five weeks before we fly to Hawaii, and I don't think it's going to be approved in time for our departure."

Charlotte responded, "What you're proposing is very hard, but there's another way that'll make it easier. Check out this information, and you make a decision." When Christina received the information in an e-mail, the Holy Spirit revealed to both of them what their next step would be. What happened next was nothing short of a miracle.

As the weeks went by, God gave Christina the ability to finish her report on time. This proved to Christina that she had been healed from dyslexia back when she was in Mozambique. She graduated with her master's degree in development only two days before their flight to Hawaii. It was hard for them to leave everything behind. Lots of things needed to be sold and given away, but they knew God had something better planned for them. They said good-bye to friends and family and left.

A few weeks after they'd settled in Hawaii, Christina began to second-guess whether or not she had heard God clearly back in Australia. She still had unanswered questions about Daniel's American residency. She called the hotlines again to ask more questions. This time, she spoke to a woman named Leslie, who was amazed at how fast their first petition had been approved. Shocked, Leslie said, "What you're proposing is very difficult, but not impossible. But wait a minute—how did you file the first step to Daniel's residency and have it processed in a few weeks? There are people who have been waiting for nine months and still haven't been approved yet. Well, it looks like things are in your favor."

A few months later, Christina called the hotline again. She started explaining her situation. The representative cut off Christina and said, "Wait—haven't I spoken with you before?"

Christina replied, "Yeah! Leslie?"

"Yeah! Whoa! This is so crazy! How did this happen? The chances of both of us talking again were slim to none!" Christina knew this was the extra confirmation she needed that the timing of their move to the United States was God's will.

There were difficulties in being a newly married couple that had just moved to the United States. Together, they learned how to persevere through trials, trust God on a deeper level, and grow in love. In everything they did, God never let them down.

After almost a year and a half of living in the United States, they both felt the Lord telling them that it was time to go back to Australia to spend time with Daniel's family. They didn't know what was coming next, but God had a reason for them to go back to Australia. While in Australia, Christina met up with her friend Elizabeth, and they prophesied over each other. Elizabeth said, "Christina, you need to go to Sacramento, and it has something to do with ministry." Elizabeth didn't know that God had told Daniel and Christina to move to the West Coast.

They knew they needed to move to Sacramento. They didn't have all the answers, but they knew that God wanted them to build connections and serve with a local church in Sacramento. They realized that God wasn't finished confirming things with them yet. They also realized that some of the confirmation regarding their marriage was like a puzzle that would only fit after their marriage.

Daniel shared his testimony with Christina. They discovered that they had both started reading *When Heaven Invades Earth* at the same time, before even knowing each other. Christina and Elizabeth happened to live only five minutes away from Daniel before they even met him, and the day Christina had moved into Elizabeth's house had also been Daniel's birthday. The love of God never fails. God not only knows the desires of our heart better than we do, but He also wants to fulfill the desires of our heart *more* than we do.

❖

When my friends Daniel and Christina shared their testimony with me, it changed my life. As I have experienced firsthand, relationships are messy, but they're always worth it, as long as I choose to see the gold in the middle of the mess. As I look back in my life at all of my failed relationships, I can say that I've learned a lot. I believe that we become like the people we hang around. That is one reason why I love hanging out with Daniel and Christina—they don't allow what happens to them to define them. Marriage is a gift from God, and the devil will do everything he can to convince many of us that we will never be married. The enemy will also try to convince married people that they've made a mistake, but the truth is that when God joins two people together in marriage, it's never a mistake. *So they are no longer two, but one flesh. Therefore what God has joined together, let no one separate* (Matthew 19:6). As we can see through Daniel and Christina's testimony, love doesn't always come the way we expect, but if we endure through the process, it'll always be better than we expect.

CHAPTER 11

The Sword That Cuts Also Heals

"The fear of the Lord is the beginning of wisdom, the beginning of wisdom is the end of hope deferred, and hope restored paints a picture of a destiny waiting to unfold."

Sonship versus Entitlement

In 1 Corinthians, the Apostle Paul says that love does not boast, it isn't proud, it isn't rude, and it isn't self-seeking. Being sons and daughters of Daddy God doesn't mean we deserve anything. Sonship isn't about entitlement; it's about stewarding an inheritance. There is a healthy fear of the Lord that sons and daughters of God need to have in order to fully operate in the authority God has given to them. In Matthew 27:50–53, regarding Jesus's death and what happened afterward, Scripture says, *And when Jesus had cried out again in a loud voice, he gave up his spirit. At that moment the curtain of the temple was torn in two from top to bottom. The earth shook, the rocks split, and the tombs broke open. The bodies of many holy people who had died were raised to life. They came out of the tombs after Jesus's resurrection and went into the holy city and appeared to many people.* If I were around when that happened, I would have a little bit more than just "respect" for God! The fear of the Lord is the beginning of wisdom, the beginning of wisdom is the end of hope deferred, and hope restored paints a picture of a destiny waiting to unfold. It's not a fear that scares us into a lifestyle of perpetual paralysis; it's a fear that keeps us in a place of humility so He can exalt us into a place of influence. The fear of the Lord is not the same as the fear of man. It's not a frightening, anxiety-driven fear; it's a fear that takes us to a promotion without leading us to entitlement.

In 2006 I started working at my first job as an automotive lube tech. Since it was an entry-level position, I ended up doing all the dirty work nobody else wanted to do. Two years later, in 2008, I was promoted to customer-service advisor. Six years after that, in 2014, I was promoted again to a lead service advisor with managerial responsibilities.

After that, I started working at a new job with a new position, thinking my new position would take me even higher up the corporate ladder. But instead of being promoted in my new position, I actually got demoted to doing something similar to what I started doing nine years ago. What's the point? Hard work, apart from colaboring with God, never pays off—and it's not supposed to.

I can work *extremely* hard my entire life to attain wealth and climb to the top of the corporate ladder, but wealth and titles can all be lost in a second, and many times for reasons that are out of our control. Entitlement is the evil stepsister of sonship. Being children of God doesn't mean we're entitled to receive rewards based on what we do; it means we will be promoted in due time because of what He did.

The last shall be first and the first shall be last is what Matthew 20:16 says, and I believe when we position our thoughts to align with that reality, that's when heaven comes and changes our reality. The fear of the Lord is not a fear that casts out love; it's a fear that purifies love until it reveals fruit that will cultivate love.

The gifts of the Spirit are not rewards for good behavior. They are an inheritance from a good Father. What we inherit as sons and daughters of God has nothing to do with who we are apart from Him; it has everything to do with who we are *because* of Him. The difference between an inheritance and entitlement is that an inheritance is something you get whether you deserve it or not. Entitlement is the belief that you get something because you think you deserve it. If anyone should be entitled to anything, it should be Jesus Christ, and even He didn't operate in that spirit. Jesus came down to earth as God in the flesh to show us what love looks like in the form of sacrifice. Jesus didn't deserve to die on a cross, He didn't deserve to be born in a manger used to feed wild animals, and He didn't deserve to ride a donkey into town. He lived a life He didn't deserve so that He could give us an abundant life that we don't deserve. The year 2012 was big for me because the Lord started using me to minister to people through visions, words of knowledge, and healing. It was very disturbing to me that during that time, I still struggled with sexual sin, outbursts of anger, and false humility.

I didn't understand how I could continue to operate in the gifts of the Holy Spirit with those problems still in control of my life. Then the Lord spoke to me and reminded me that His gifts and callings are irrevocable (read Romans 11:29). When God gives us gifts, we can either use them to destroy people or empower them. Operating in the power of God without the love of God does not reveal the character of God. After I processed what the Holy Spirit was telling me, I knew I needed to change. I didn't change because I wanted to start doing the right thing. I decided to change because I wanted to start doing the God thing. A gift is never something that can be earned. If these gifts could be earned, they wouldn't be called "the gifts of the Spirit." They would be called "the rewards of the Spirit."

To think of His gifts as rewards is to say that what Jesus did on the cross wasn't enough and that we still need to earn things we believe He never fully paid the price for. We don't receive gifts from God because we are worthy of them; we receive His gifts because He's our Daddy, and that's just what He does. We don't receive His love because of anything we can do to earn it; we receive His love because He *is* love. We aren't amazing because of who we are; we're amazing because of who we are *in* Him.

The Healing Cut

For the Word of God is alive and active. Sharper than any double-edged sword, it penetrates even to dividing soul and spirit, joints and marrow; it judges the thoughts and attitudes of the heart (Hebrews 4:12). The sword that divides the soul and spirit also brings healing through the Book that reveals His Spirit (Ephesians 6:17). One of the reasons I believe it is so difficult for many people to embrace change is because of their fear of recovery. Sometimes God heals cancer supernaturally, but other times He heals cancer with a scalpel used by the hands of a doctor (read Mark 2:17). Christine Caine, an

Australian evangelist and international speaker, once said, "The pain of recovery is often far greater than the pain of the injury. If you embrace the pain, you will eventually embrace your healing." The fear of the Lord brings great humility and transformation through the process of embracing the pain of recovery. In a metaphorical sense, I believe God holds a scalpel in His hands, looks at us living in our pain, and says, "Come here." He's a good Father who cuts out the cancer designed to kill us so that He can create a testimony that will promote us.

In my early teenage years and into my early twenties, I was never a regular drinker, but when I did drink, I always got drunk and blacked out. My struggle with drinking started when I turned twenty-one years old, which is the legal drinking age in America. On the evening of my twenty-first birthday, I went to a bar with some friends and family. I drank two full glasses of long island iced tea and a couple of shots of some other drinks that even people who were sober wouldn't drink. No one forced me to drink that night; I drank of my own will, just for fun—at least, that's what I thought. I see drinking too much the same way I see smoking weed, sniffing cocaine, or indulging in unhealthy sexual addiction. Once I experienced a temporary high that made me feel good, I wanted more.

After getting drunk a few more times, I realized that I could use alcohol to hide my depression. When I drank, things that normally bothered me didn't bother me anymore until I sobered up. One morning I had a hangover that was so bad that I was just as drunk in the morning as I was the night prior. The problem was that I had to go to work. Still drunk, I got in my car and drove an hour and a half to my job. As I got onto the freeway, I turned my head to check and see if there were any cars in the lane next to mine before I changed lanes. When I turned my head back to the road ahead of me, I could feel everything spinning. I was so afraid because there was nothing I could do to stop the spinning. I pulled into the slow lane to be safe. Not too long after, I saw a police car go right by me.

I thought the officer might have noticed that I was drunk, but he didn't, and he kept driving. The fear that gripped me was almost too much for me to bear. When I finally got to work, I was still buzzed. The buzz continued to last all day, but no one seemed to notice because I avoided talking to people as much as possible. I never got a DUI, and I never got fired for being drunk at work, but that scary experience showed me how dangerous my drinking problem actually was. That morning I drove drunk, I could have crashed into an innocent family, I could have gotten a DUI, I could have lost my job, or I could have recklessly killed myself. Despite everything that happened that day, I believe God was protecting me, even in my sin. For a lot of people, an experience like that would have been enough to get them to stop drinking, but it didn't stop me.

My problem with drinking continued for a few years until one night, Jesus revealed Himself to me in a way that changed me from that day forward. That particular night while I was driving home, I was very depressed and uncertain of the direction of my life. I stopped at a store to buy alcohol. When I got home, I drank the entire bottle within minutes. After about ten minutes, I could feel the effect. I felt numb to my emotions, which is exactly what I wanted to happen. As I sat in my bed with a blank look on my face,

I simply closed my eyes and allowed the alcohol to take me to a place where there was no pain. I heard worship music playing in my head. I opened my eyes and felt ashamed. "I don't want to hear worship music right now!" I thought, but I couldn't make the music stop.

Then I heard the Lord say, "I love you, son." Tears streamed down my face. I couldn't believe God loved me in that moment. The Lord also told me how much my drinking was hurting our relationship. I didn't know who I was in Christ at that time, and I only "didn't drink" because I wanted to follow the rules of Christianity. That day the Holy Spirit gave me the power to stop allowing drunkenness to control my life. Though the Holy Spirit transformed my life that day and removed the hold that drinking had over me, I was left with a void that took many years for Him to fill. Once I stopped going to alcohol to drown out my sorrows, I learned how to go to Jesus to heal the pain. This meant meeting with or calling a friend whenever I was feeling depressed, sending a group text, or strengthening myself in the Lord by talking with Jesus in my secret place.

Alcohol was my crutch whenever I experienced pain. It made me feel better for a moment, but in the end, it only slowed me down. Recovery looks like taking off the crutches and starting to walk again; trusting God when everybody around you says you're crazy; and, most importantly, allowing the Holy Spirit to cut out the thorn in your side to allow His love to heal the pain from your past.

Our God, who plans to throw the devil into a lake of fire and brimstone to burn forever, is the same God that sent His son Jesus to die on a cross so that every person has a chance, through His resurrection, to live forever (read Revelations 20:10 and John 3:16). The glory of the Lord is so spectacular that if we saw Him face-to-face in human form, His glory would kill us (Exodus 33:20); this is what I believe the fear of the Lord looks like. It looks like a love that is so spectacular, so pure, and so holy that only our inner spirit, fully intertwined with His Spirit, is capable of seeing God face-to-face without repercussions. This is why I believe Jesus reveals Himself to us, in human form, through visions, dreams, and angelic visitations.

The sword of the Spirit, the Word of God, is designed to cut off what brings death, so that a tree that brings life can take root. Our God doesn't need to choose between being a lover or a fighter—He is both. He is a warrior who uses His sword to fight our battles, but He is also a lover whose heart cries out for intimacy and relationship with us (read Exodus 15:3 and 1 John 4:8). The fear of man casts out love, but the fear of the Lord purifies love. If you live by the sword of man, you will die by the sword of man, but if you live by the sword of the Spirit, you will live forever in the love of a good Father.

CHAPTER 12

Sustaining a Culture of Revival

"Revival is initiated with passion, it's sustained from a place of rest, and it spreads by the power of His love."

The Importance of Rest

We were created for relationships, we thrive because of relationships, and we do revival from relationships. I believe the revival we'll see in this generation will be started with people who are hungry, but it will be cultivated through people who are healthy, and healthy people know how to rest. Revival is initiated with passion, but it's cultivated from a place of rest. One of the biggest problems is that a lot of us think revival is something that starts externally, but revival starts as an inside job. We can't steward revival around us if we refuse to cultivate it within us. To steward an external revival, it must flow outwardly from a pure, healed, and whole heart. I believe initiating revival looks like stepping outside of our comfort zone—in other words, "getting out of the boat." But stewarding revival looks like building a legacy for others to follow. As I mentioned in chapter 11, advancing the kingdom of God on earth has nothing to do with striving and working really hard but with resting in His presence knowing that He's got it covered. A lot of us have a problem with resting because we are naturally wired from the day we were born to work hard so that we can receive a compliment or a reward. Heaven isn't something we need to convince people of; it's something we need to release from within. Luke 17:21 (KJV) says, *The kingdom of God is within you.* As believers, we carry the reality of heaven within us to release to a broken world that longs for an encounter with the love of the Father.

In 2014 I was working for an automotive-repair shop as a customer-service advisor. Around that time, I had been working there for about eight and a half years. Things at work had been going well until October. One sunny afternoon, while I was writing a work order for one of my customers, my manager cracked open his office door and waved me over to his office. I knew something wasn't right, judging by the look on his face. After I finished helping my customer, I walked over to my manager's office, opened the door, and sat down in anticipation for what he was about to tell me. My manager, Jared, looked me in the eyes and said, "Ernesto, the reason you're here is because I want you to know that our company is really struggling financially, and I was told by upper management that I will need to lay off about six or seven of you. The reason I called you into my office first is because I want you to know that you are not one of the people we're going to lay off. Because your sales numbers are exceptional, we want to offer you a full-time position."

Shocked, I said, "Wow, that's crazy. I'm a little nervous about what's going to happen next. If I accept this full-time position, how many service advisors will I be working with?"

"If you accept the position, you will be our only service advisor five days out of the week."

Still bewildered, I said, "Wow, that's going to be intense, but OK, I'll take the position." After the company laid off all of the other service advisors, I started working full time for fifty hours a week. After about two months of being the only full-time service advisor, the stress was starting to get to me. Several days out of the week, I would come in at 8:00 a.m., and there would already be eight customers parked in front of the company, waiting for us to open the store. One particular day, I remember there were about ten people standing in line waiting for me to help them. One customer was angry with me because the tires he wanted were cheaper online than the in-store price. Another was angry because it had been three hours, and I didn't update him on the status of his vehicle. Yet another customer yelled at me over the phone because I didn't have any time to answer the phones, and the list goes on and on.

As the day went on, I remember feeling dizzy on the sales floor. When that happened, I said to all of the customers, "Hey, guys, I need to take care of something in the back for a while. Somebody will be with all of you shortly." As I walked to the employees-only room, the customers glared at me as though I were the devil. My head was pounding so much that I felt like I was going to pass out. I made my way to the break room and drank a lot of water and laid my head on the table to rest. I didn't have anyone to help me, and I didn't know what else to do. While my head was on the table, I could still hear the phone ringing. I wasn't sure if the phones were actually ringing or if it was just my imagination—it was hard to tell the difference at that point.

I heard someone say, "Ernesto!"

I looked up, and Jared said to me, "Hey, are you OK?"

"I'm feeling really weak and tired, and I couldn't take it anymore."

"Is there anyone on the sales floor?"

"No, I'm sorry. I'm so exhausted."

"That's OK; don't worry about it. Just get plenty of rest. I'm back from lunch."

It was that day I realized that the stress of the job was affecting me physically, but I continued working, and I continued striving. A few days after that happened, in November of 2014, I was on the sales floor talking with one of my managers. All of a sudden, I felt intense pain in my chest. The pain was so intense that I couldn't breathe. I looked at my manager with a confused look on my face, and he said, "Are you all right?"

"I don't know. My chest hurts *really* bad, and I can't breathe."

Jared was concerned. "I think you need to take a break. Take as long as you want. We want to make sure you're OK."

With my right hand pressed against my chest, I slowly walked to the break room. Every step I took was so excruciatingly painful that I wondered whether or not I'd even make it to the break room to sit down. Eventually, I got there and sat down to rest. The pain started to subside.

I didn't know what was wrong with me, but I knew that the pain seemed to get worse whenever I would take a deep breath or try to stand up. The pain was so bad that I wondered if I was having a heart attack. "A heart attack at twenty-seven years old? No way!" I thought. As I sat there, I had visions of my tombstone, and I could feel my body shutting down. It had gotten so serious that I finally decided to check myself into the emergency room.

Several minutes later, Jared walked into the break room and said, "Hey, Ernesto—how are you feeling, man?"

"I still feel the same. I think I need to clock out and go to the emergency room."

Surprised, Jared replied, "Wow, that bad, huh? Well, you need to take care of yourself, so if you need to go to emergency room, go ahead and clock out. I hope you get better soon." I drove myself to the hospital and walked toward the entrance.

Because I didn't have medical insurance, I was reluctant to go inside for treatment, but I knew it needed to be done. Suddenly, I heard the Holy Spirit say, *Try to take one more really deep breath before you go in there.* I stopped and took a *really* deep breath. As I breathed out, I felt something pop in my chest. I tried to breathe, and everything was back to normal. I didn't have any more pain. Just to make sure I was really OK, I jumped up and down and breathed heavily, and the pain in my chest was completely gone. Relieved, I walked back to my car. I started driving back to work, but something in my conscious didn't feel right. I pulled over on the side of the road and prayed. I said to God, "I can't do this anymore. I don't want to go back. God, what do you want me to do? Should I quit?"

God said, *I told you to quit a long time ago, but you didn't listen to me; it didn't have to come to this.* I started to cry. After I finished processing with God, I picked up the phone and called my manager.

While I held the phone to my ear, listening to the sound of the dial tone, it seemed like the whole world slowed down. "After eight and a half years working for this company, and this is how it all ends? What's going to happen next? I don't even have a job lined up," I thought.

Jared answered the phone. "Hello?"

"Hey, man, I'm so sorry, but I can't take this anymore. I'm just calling to let you know that I quit. This is just too much."

"I totally understand; don't even worry about it. Well, it was good working with you. Good luck in all of your ventures in life, and make sure you get plenty of rest."

"I know the way I'm quitting isn't ideal, and I'm sorry about that. But can I use you as a reference when I apply for new jobs?"

"Absolutely, man. With things the way they've been here lately, I'm not even sure I'll be working here much longer. But in the meantime, you can totally use me as a reference."

Surprised, I replied, "Thanks so much!"

At the time I quit my job, I had about $3,000 in my account. I had been planning on using that money to go back to Mozambique in 2015 (as I mentioned in chapter 9). But my plans changed when I found myself unemployed for the first time since I was eighteen years old. For the first few weeks after I quit, I didn't know what to do. I had been so used to a daily routine that I didn't even know who I was anymore. I had been so used to striving and working really hard that I didn't know what it was like to rest. I fell into a depression. I snapped myself out of it and prayed, asking God what to do. I heard the Lord say, *I want you to apply for jobs on Saturdays from 8:00 a.m. to 6:00 p.m. I want you to spend time in my presence the other six days, and I want you to meet with a friend at least four evenings out of the week.* I started doing as He said. In the meantime, my car broke down, and it cost me about $1,500 to have it repaired. Finally, after about two months, I only had about $250 in my bank account.

I said to myself, "If God didn't tell me to quit my job, I'm about to find out within the next few weeks." By the end of January 2015, I met with another friend. During our conversation, my friend Charles smiled and said, "I feel like the Lord told me to give this to you. Don't open this envelope until you get home."

I was surprised. "Thank you, brother!" When I got home, I opened the envelope, and there was $100.

About a week later, a stranger from church walked up to me after service and said, "Excuse me, I'm Brian, and I feel like the Lord wants us to meet for coffee sometime."

"Sure, brother. Let's exchange numbers!"

Later that week, we met for coffee, and in the middle of our conversation, he said to me, "I feel like the Lord wants me to give you this money." Brian reached into his wallet and slid a wad of cash across the table. After I thanked him and returned home, I counted it, and there was over $300. Neither Charles nor Brian knew that I was unemployed.

About a week later, I watched a Heidi Baker video about resting in God's presence. Afterward, I started soaking with God and spending time in worship with Him. Later that afternoon, my phone rang. When I answered, the woman on the other end of the phone said, "Hello! Ernesto, right?"

I replied, "Yes, that's right."

"OK, well, we've been reviewing job applications, and we really like yours a lot. We would like you to come in for an interview tomorrow. Would that work?"

I was excited. "Sure, that works!" At the interview, the woman hired me on the spot for a job in which I would be making the same amount of money as my last job, but I wouldn't have to work as hard.

❀

It was during the time that I was unemployed that God completed stripped me down until all I needed was Him. It wasn't until I learned how to rest in His presence that my breakthrough came. Revival is initiated with passion, it's sustained from a place of rest, and it spreads by the power of His love. In 1 Corinthians 13:1–3, it says, *If I speak in the tongues of men or of angels, but do not have love, I am only a resounding gong or a clanging cymbal. If I have the gift of prophecy and can fathom all mysteries and all knowledge, and if I have a faith that can move mountains, but do not have love, I am nothing. If I give all I possess to the poor and give over my body to hardship that I may boast, but do not have love, I gain nothing.* It's by demonstrating the power of the kingdom that we fully preach the Gospel (Romans 15:19), but without love, there wouldn't be a Gospel. Without love, nothing matters.

www.ingramcontent.com/pod-product-compliance
Lightning Source LLC
Chambersburg PA
CBHW022336280326
41934CB00006B/650